W9-AWG-532

Praise for

GABRIELLE BERNSTEIN
AND SUPER ATTRACTOR

"Those of us who have no doubt that consciousness is the fundamental reality which conceives, constructs, governs, and becomes that which we call physical reality have no doubt that in every moment the world is a mirror of our inner state of being. This book explains with elegant simplicity and practical steps how you can be the author of your life story and manifest your deepest desires and cherished dreams."
— Deepak Chopra, M.D.

"Gabrielle is the real thing. I respect her work immensely."
— Dr. Wayne Dyer

Named "a new thought leader" by Oprah's SuperSoul Sunday

SUPER ATTRACTOR

ALSO BY GABRIELLE BERNSTEIN

Books

Super Attractor Journal*

Judgment Detox

Judgment Detox Journal

The Universe Has Your Back*

The Universe Has Your Back Journal*

Miracles Now*

May Cause Miracles

Spirit Junkie

Add More ~ing to Your Life

Cards

Super Attractor: A 52-Card Deck*

The Universe Has Your Back: A 52-Card Deck*

Miracles Now: A 62-Card Deck*

*Available from Hay House
Please visit:

Hay House USA: www.hayhouse.com®
Hay House Australia: www.hayhouse.com.au
Hay House UK: www.hayhouse.co.uk
Hay House India: www.hayhouse.co.in

***

SUPER ATTRACTOR

METHODS FOR MANIFESTING A LIFE BEYOND YOUR WILDEST DREAMS

GABRIELLE BERNSTEIN

HAY HOUSE, INC.

Carlsbad, California • New York City

London • Sydney • New Delhi

Copyright © 2019 by Gabrielle Bernstein

Published in the United States by: Hay House, Inc.: www.hayhouse.com®
• *Published in Australia by:* Hay House Australia Pty. Ltd.: www.hay house.com.au • *Published in the United Kingdom by:* Hay House UK, Ltd.: www.hayhouse.co.uk • *Published in India by:* Hay House Publishers India: www.hayhouse.co.in

Cover design: Tracey Edelstein • *Interior design:* Nick C. Welch

All rights reserved. No part of this book may be reproduced by any mechanical, photographic, or electronic process, or in the form of a phonographic recording; nor may it be stored in a retrieval system, transmitted, or otherwise be copied for public or private use—other than for "fair use" as brief quotations embodied in articles and reviews—without prior written permission of the publisher.

The author of this book does not dispense medical advice or prescribe the use of any technique as a form of treatment for physical, emotional, or medical problems without the advice of a physician, either directly or indirectly. The intent of the author is only to offer information of a general nature to help you in your quest for emotional, physical, and spiritual well-being. In the event you use any of the information in this book for yourself, the author and the publisher assume no responsibility for your actions.

Library of Congress has cataloged the earlier edition as follows:

Names: Bernstein, Gabrielle, author.
Title: Super attractor : manifest the life you want / Gabrielle Bernstein.
Description: Carlsbad, California : Hay House, Inc., [2019] | Includes
   bibliographical references and index.
Identifiers: LCCN 2019018529 | ISBN 9781401957162 (hardcover : alk.
paper)
Subjects: LCSH: Self-realization. | Self-realization—Religious aspects. |
   Spirituality.
Classification: LCC BF637.S4 B4748 2019 | DDC 158.1—dc23 LC record
available at https://lccn.loc.gov/2019018529

Tradepaper ISBN: 978-1-4019-5719-3
E-book ISBN: 978-1-4019-5717-9
Autographed Edition ISBN: 978-1-4019-5915-9

10 9 8 7 6 5 4 3 2 1
1st edition, September 2019
2nd edition, February 2021

Printed in the United States of America

For my son, Oliver.

CONTENTS

INTRODUCTION

You Are a Super Attractor

I've always known that there is a nonphysical presence beyond my visible sight. All my life I've intuitively tuned in to it and used it as a source for good. I've tapped into this unlimited presence of power to heal my body, support my relationships, guide my career in the service of others, and attract my greatest desires.

There are many names for this type of spiritual presence. I refer to it interchangeably as the Universe, God, spirit, inner guidance, love, and other terms too. You may have your own word that resonates with you. Or maybe you're new to spirituality and don't yet have a vocabulary around it. It doesn't matter. What we call it is irrelevant. Connecting to it is imperative. The very fact that you are reading this book right now is evidence that you have listened, consciously or unconsciously, to divine guidance that led you here, and you are willing to claim that connection.

I honor you for your willingness. Claiming my connection to the presence of this power has directed the course of my life. The simple choice to tune in to this source of love has helped me recover from addiction, heal PTSD, undo fearful beliefs, and live with clear purpose.

My connection to the presence of love has been my guide, my protector, and my partner in the co-creation of my life. Living my life in daily devotion to this nonphysical source of power has made me a Super Attractor.

Being a Super Attractor means that what I believe is what I receive. I can co-create the world I want to see by aligning with good-feeling emotions and directing them toward my desires. I can tap into an unlimited source of creative energy to contribute inspired ideas, offer wisdom, receive abundance, and feel free. And best of all, I can harness this power into a force for good in the world.

Being a Super Attractor doesn't mean I haven't had to face very real challenges. But I can see clearly how my struggles have been part of a bigger plan to help me strengthen my faith in my Super Attractor connection. I've chosen to perceive hard life experiences as spiritual assignments for growth and healing. I've accepted that nothing happens by accident. And I know that as long as I remember I'm a Super Attractor, I will be able to accept difficult experiences as opportunities to fine-tune my inner power and get closer to consciousness. The tough stuff offers me a chance to shine the crystal that is me. Being a Super Attractor doesn't mean everything is perfect—but it does mean that I show up for life with faith, no matter what. Claiming my Super Attractor power has helped me to move through rough times with much more grace, honesty, and compassion than I otherwise would.

Living my life in this way has brought me what I desire most: freedom. I feel free knowing that there is an ever-present energy of love within me and around me. I'm free knowing that I'm always being guided and that I have the power to co-create the world I want to see. Freedom is the greatest gift of all. Nothing holds me back. I no longer play small. For more than a decade, I've lived, loved, and taught with this freedom. Freedom has given me the experience of being an untethered force of light in the world.

When you align yourself with your Super Attractor energy, you no longer feel blocked by fear. You remember that you are a spirit having a human experience. The spirit within you is the presence of inspiration, joy, and the truth of who you are. When you practice these steps, you remember that you are a wise, powerful, healthy, and holy spirit. When you accept this, you can be free. The feeling of freedom is inevitable when you attune your energy to the presence of your truth. You may not stay connected to this truth all the time, but the more often you turn to it, the easier it will be to feel free.

As a spiritual teacher, I have witnessed hundreds of thousands of people throughout the world begin to wake up to the presence of freedom within. I see these transformations daily. But while that awakening is beautiful, it isn't enough. Too often we treat it as the end point, when it's really just the beginning. We may know that we can feel better and therefore attract more, but we must go further and fully embody that truth in order to be free. Embodying this truth begins by undoing the belief systems of fear that block us from being Super Attractors. We must be willing and committed to change the way we think, act, and live.

In my case, I didn't have to go out and find this connection; I just had to slow down and remember it. I've devoted my life to the process of slowing down and realigning with the presence of inner power. With each meditation, I vibrate at a higher frequency; with each prayer, I surrender to a power greater than myself. My dedication to the spiritual realm has given me the freedom I desire. I am not exceptional. You have this connection too, and claiming it is both fun and easy. In this book, I want to share with you how to connect to that power.

I want you to know this: you are a Super Attractor.

If that feels strange to you right now, that's okay. But I know that by the time you finish this book, you will claim that power with total confidence and ease. You will know beyond a shadow of a doubt that you are a Super Attractor.

In 2016, I published a book called *The Universe Has Your Back: Transform Fear to Faith*. Readers throughout the world followed the book's lessons to strengthen their faith in the Universe. They reclaimed their connection to a higher power and restored their faith in love. When I was preparing to write a new book, I intuitively knew that it was time to take these teachings to the next level. This book is that next step. With the practices outlined in the coming chapters, I'm going to push the spiritual envelope to teach you how to fine-tune your spiritual connection to effortlessly attract what you want into your life. If you haven't read *The Universe Has Your Back*, don't sweat it. It's not a prerequisite. Trust that you were guided here first for a reason.

You may already be on a spiritual path. You may already practice manifesting and live by the Law of Attraction. Or these concepts may be completely new to you. Either way, this book will help them become second nature. Throughout the book I will share my own personal methods for aligning with your Super Attractor presence. Some of these practices have been greatly influenced by my teachers Abraham-Hicks, Dr. Wayne W. Dyer, and the metaphysical text *A Course in Miracles*. But my greatest teacher of all has been my life experience. Each day offers new opportunities to get closer to the Universe and strengthen my Super Attractor power. Each life challenge offers new miracles and lessons. Throughout the book I'll call on my own personal examples of what it's like to live in alignment and be a Super Attractor.

RECLAIMING YOUR SUPER ATTRACTOR POWER

To master your Super Attractor power, you must start by understanding how you've likely become disconnected from it. In nearly 15 years as a spiritual teacher, I've gained a very clear understanding of the common ways people misuse and block this power. I expect you'll recognize yourself in some (or all) of the most common types.

DID YOU FORGET YOUR POWER?

Even a person on a spiritual path can forget that they're a Super Attractor. It's all too easy to get sucked into the fear-based stories of the world and weaken your faith. When fear takes over, you go into a kind of comatose state. You literally forget who you really are. You build up belief systems of separation, lack, judgment, and negativity. All these false perceptions deny your inner power and block your Super Attractor power. This book will be a wake-up call to remind you of who you really are. Just by opening to this introduction, you've begun to wake up and remember.

ARE YOU MANIC MANIFESTING?

There are many people who read personal growth books, attend seminars, meditate, pray . . . and still feel stuck. I hear this often: "Gabby, I'm doing everything right, but I still feel so off. I'm praying, meditating, and using positive affirmations, but I'm still not attracting what I want. What's wrong?!"

What's wrong is that they are doing what I call "manic manifesting." These folks have faith in the Universe, and lots of spiritual tools, but they are energetically blocking their connection. They've been playing tricks with the Universe rather than aligning with their true power. Manic manifesting happens when someone has all the spiritual tools and jargon but forgets the most important part of attracting: to tune in to the Universe. You can say affirmations, pray, and meditate every day and still not attract because your energy is out of alignment. Instead of allowing yourself to receive, you want to "get." This book will teach you that the most important element of manifesting with the Universe is to embody the energy of love. If you identify as a manic manifester, you're in the right place! In this book I'll hook you up with a whole new way of being.

ARE YOU A PUSHER?

Pushers are people who try to push and control to reach their goals and feel safe. They believe that the more they do, the more they'll achieve. They're trying to "make things happen" rather than allowing themselves to attract naturally. They've forgotten that there is support beyond their own action and will. Pushers believe that they have to make things happen, and aligning and receiving guidance don't come into the equation. They've forgotten where their true power lies. This is a common characteristic, and it's one that many cultures often seem to reward. Pushers have a fear-based belief that if they're not super productive, nothing will happen for them. Little do they know that their pushy energy is blocking their capacity to attract! The Universe doesn't respond as well to frantic energy. Rather, the Universe vibrates at a positive frequency, and to co-create with it, your energy must align with that frequency.

The practices in this book will help you slow down, be still, and allow. I will teach you the art of allowing so that you can stop pushing, feel secure, and start receiving naturally.

DOES FEAR HAVE YOU IN A HEADLOCK?

Each day brings new opportunities to lean toward fear or lean into love. While we always have a choice, we often (quite unconsciously) default to fear. We choose fear in many ways, from the TV we watch to the conversations we have to the thoughts we entertain. The presence of fear is a sure sign we've disconnected from the loving presence of the Universe.

Throughout the book I'll offer you practical tools and spiritual principles to undo fear and reclaim love. Undoing fear doesn't have to be hard. In fact, it can be much easier than you've ever imagined. Get ready to create radical shifts fast!

DO YOU JUDGE?

Judging, comparing, attacking, and seeing ourselves as separate from others all disconnect us from the Universe. If you identify as a judgmental person (judging others or yourself), take a moment to acknowledge how it makes you feel. Be honest and gentle with yourself as you do this. While you may feel justified in your judgment or try to rationalize it, it's undeniable how negative it makes you feel. Being a Super Attractor is about feeling good, and in this book I'll give you lots of amazing tools and spiritual practices to help you cultivate joy and have fun! As you become willing to release your judgment and choose compassion and peace instead, you will reconnect to your power.

These are just a few of the common ways we block our Super Attractor power. The good news is that your power never left you! You simply forgot about it. This book will guide you to recognize it, claim it, use it to attract what you want, and be a force for good in the world.

Let me guide you to become a Super Attractor through powerful steps explained in the upcoming chapters. These chapters will include spiritual methods and lessons that build on each other so that by the end you will have fully claimed your power. While each method in this book can be applied independently, I've placed them in an order that has a cumulative effect. Practice each method as presented so that you can get the most out of this transformational process. You may find that some lessons resonate with you more than others. That's okay! Once you've gone through each chapter, you can then apply the tools interchangeably and at your own pace. Most importantly—have fun! The more fun you have, the stronger your Super Attractor power becomes. Fun turns you into a magnet for miracles.

And here's the promise: When you accept that you are a Super Attractor, life gets awesome! You feel joyful, inspired, purposeful, and empowered. You'll no longer feel the need to control, compare, or push, and you'll settle into a sense of ease. Best of all, you'll become a powerful example for others—and you'll vibrate at such a high, loving frequency that your energy will be felt far and wide.

Here's how the book breaks down:

CHAPTER 1: THE UNIVERSE ALWAYS DELIVERS

Every thought you have is a message you send to the Universe. The Universe is always saying YES to your thoughts, energy, and emotions. Therefore, what you put out you will receive back—whether you want it or not. In Chapter 1 I'll guide you to bring awareness to what you're asking for. I'll help you see how you're often asking for what you *don't* want, and I'll show you how you can consciously clarify your requests to the Universe. This is an imperative step toward being a Super Attractor because it establishes a clear dialogue with the Universe. In this chapter I'll teach you my method for tapping into your Super Attractor power instead of following the voice of fear, and I'll show you how to make it a habit that's easy to sustain.

CHAPTER 2: IT'S GOOD TO FEEL GOOD

One of the biggest blocks to being a Super Attractor is our resistance to feeling good. We've all grown far more comfortable in a state of fear than in a place of joy and faith. We've learned to rely on fear as a way of protecting ourselves from being disappointed, hurt, or triggered. We've become so accustomed to the fearful projections of the world that we don't trust that things can be good. Unconsciously we feel that if we focus on everything good, we will lose control and be unsafe. In Chapter 2 you'll learn how to change your thoughts about your fears and begin to make feeling good a priority. This step prepares you for the manifesting to come because in order to attract all that's good, you must first believe you are worthy of it. The exercises in Chapter 2 will help you welcome worthiness and happiness and prepare you to claim all that you will attract.

CHAPTER 3: THERE'S MORE THAN ENOUGH TO GO AROUND

The fear of not having enough is a major block to your Super Attractor power. The energy of lack causes us to vibrate at a low frequency, repelling the very things we want and thereby creating more lack.

Therefore, in Chapter 3 I'll teach you my method for transcending lack and comparison through positive intention. This practice guides you to pray for others to have more of what you want for yourself. You'll quickly see how wanting more for others puts you into an energy of abundance! It feels good to want others to feel good. The simple practice of wishing for others to receive will put you into an energy of receptivity, and this feeling of abundance will rapidly begin to attract more of what you want into your life. When you genuinely want others to be abundant, your good fortune will multiply.

CHAPTER 4: HAVE FUN ALONG THE WAY

In Chapter 4 I'll wake you up to the awesome power of fun! Joy is the ultimate creator and the most powerful vibration we can embody. When you calibrate your energy to the experience of joy, you become a magnet for whatever you think about. In this chapter I'll teach you a method that will help you quickly move from negative, low-level thoughts and energy to a more positive state. I'll guide you to trust in the power of your thoughts and energy to help you navigate life's challenges so you can show up for life in a state of joy. Through the practices in Chapter 4, you'll see that when you lean toward joy, you are led!

CHAPTER 5: LIFT THE VEIL

In Chapter 5 I'll guide you to understand and embrace your true power. It isn't some credential, status, or achievement. I'll show you that your true power lies in your capacity to tune in to the energy of love and the inner vision of light. *A Course in Miracles* says, "Miracles are seen in light." In this chapter you'll learn what it means to see in light and to bring light with you wherever you go. I'll also teach you my Meditation for Lifting the Veil, in which you transcend the energy of this world and step into a place of love.

CHAPTER 6: INVISIBLE GUIDANCE IS AVAILABLE TO YOU

In Chapter 6 I'm going to push the metaphysical envelope and invite you to open up to new forms of guidance. In order to help you establish a spiritual relationship *of your own understanding*, I'll share my own beliefs about spiritual guides. These guides are wise, loving, and compassionate, and they can help you in every area of your life. I'll introduce you to the different kinds of spiritual guides, including angels and archangels, your Higher Self, the love of the Universe, and family members and friends who have passed on. I'll teach you how to connect with these spiritual guides and how to receive guidance and help from them.

CHAPTER 7: DO LESS AND ATTRACT MORE

As I noted before, pushing is one of the greatest blocks to being a Super Attractor. Being a Super Attractor is about strengthening your faith, tuning in to the energy of love, and allowing the Universe to catch up with your dreams. To begin the practice of allowing, we must get out of the way and let life flow so we can truly thrive as a Super Attractor.

In Chapter 7 I'll teach you how to turn over your desires to the care of the Universe or a higher power of your own understanding. The daily practice of surrendering your plans to a higher power will help you cultivate your ability to be still and embrace the present moment. In stillness we receive. You'll experience immense relief, a drop in anxiety, and a surge of energy as you stop pouring all your mental, emotional, and even physical effort into pushing, controlling, and trying to make things happen. I'll help you trust that your alignment with the Universe is enough to co-create the world you want to see.

CHAPTER 8: TAKING SPIRITUALLY ALIGNED ACTION

By Chapter 8 you will have undergone deep transformations! At this point you'll be vibrating at a Super Attractor frequency and ready to learn how to direct your powerful energy toward your desires. You'll be ready to start co-creating with the Universe through fun, creative, and eye-opening practices. I'll teach you how to clarify your desires through the power of intention. Your positive, excited intentions, combined with your free-flowing energy, will prime you to take spiritually aligned action. You'll begin to see your desires come into form in clear, concrete, and at times beautifully startling ways. In this chapter you'll get into the groovy practice of celebrating your miracle moments and manifestations!

CHAPTER 9: APPRECIATE AND APPRECIATE MORE

Once you've begun showing up for life in a joyful state and taking spiritually aligned action, you'll be ready to fully appreciate everything in your life. Appreciation dissolves all blocks to the presence of our power. When we're in a state of appreciation, we're actively creating more of what we want. We're also in an energy of acceptance and nonresistance. In the absence of resistance, we are Super Attractors.

In this chapter I'll guide you through appreciation practices that will fill your heart with excitement and enthusiasm for life! Once you access a state of appreciation, I'll guide you to reach for even more of it. When you get into the flow of appreciation, you want to create even more momentum behind it. You'll learn how to make appreciation a habit so that you can effortlessly maintain a powerful and positive point of attraction.

CHAPTER 10: LET THE UNIVERSE CATCH UP WITH YOUR DREAMS

The secret to attracting is to surrender your desire to the highest good! Chapter 10 will help you loosen your grip and rely on a higher power to show you the next right action. In this chapter you'll learn how to relax and enjoy the manifestation process! The best part of being a Super Attractor is that you don't have to figure it all out. You can direct your focus, dwell in the energy of fun, and surrender your desires to the Universe. I'll guide you to pay attention to your inner wisdom and to signs from the Universe. Above all, this chapter is about turning over your will to the care of a higher power so you can let miracles unfold naturally.

CHAPTER 11: UNWAVERING FAITH IN THE UNIVERSE

In this chapter I'll teach you how to allow the abundant love of the Universe to flow. You'll learn how to see fear as a pathway back to love, and I'll teach you techniques that will help you stay in the stream of well-being and protect your good-feeling emotions. You will claim a sense of faithful knowing, and you'll see how living with positive expectations clears the path for solutions in all situations, even the difficult ones. When we align our thoughts and energy with spiritual faith, we can expect miracles. Faith isn't hoping that God will help you; faith is *knowing* that help is on the way.

LIVING A SPIRITUAL LIFE

This text will help you to understand the importance of living in alignment with the Universe—not just dabbling in your practice when it feels convenient. I don't want your spiritual life compartmentalized and kept separate from your day-to-day experiences. I want you to live a spiritual life all the time. I want you to feel a sense of awe each day as you witness miracles unfold. I want you to feel connected to a spiritual force that you can rely on. I want you to attract what you desire and create a life filled with purpose, happiness, abundance, and peace. I want you to feel free.

Accepting that you are a Super Attractor will change everything. You'll trust that it's safe to release the past, and you'll no longer fear the future. You'll tap into an infinite source of abundance, energy, joy, and well-being. This well-being will become the norm for you, and you'll grow to embrace it as your birthright. Most importantly, you'll know intuitively how to show up for life and bring more light to the world around you.

This book is a journey of remembering where your true power lies. You'll learn how to co-create the life you want. You'll accept that life can flow, that attracting is fun, and that you don't have to work so hard to get what you want. Best of all, you'll feel good.

BECOMING A FORCE OF LOVE IN THE WORLD

Once you claim your Super Attractor power, the question then becomes: *What will you do with it?* When you feel good, you give off a presence of joy that can elevate everyone around you. By claiming your true power, you will help others do the same. The practices here will empower you to live your purpose, and they will amplify abundance, happiness, health, and peace for everyone you come into contact with and beyond. By the end of this book, you will have a greater understanding of your higher purpose. You will know how to fulfill your function: to be a force of love in the world.

It's time to claim your power. Turn to Chapter 1 and let's begin.

Chapter 1

THE UNIVERSE ALWAYS DELIVERS

I'm so psyched to be sitting at my desk writing this book! I wake up in the middle of the night thinking about all that I want to share with you. I long to get these words onto the page. I'm thrilled that you're here, and I'm equally excited for myself. You see, I need this book more than you can imagine. At a recent talk I gave, an audience member said to me, "Gabby, I'm a life coach, and I feel like a fraud. I've got a lot of fear, I obsess about the small stuff, and I'm still working out a lot of personal issues. How can I help others manifest their dreams when I'm going through such a hard time?" I laughed and said, "Honey, I'm writing my seventh spiritual book, and I'm still a head case!" In that moment I admitted to myself and a public audience that I was out of alignment with my Super Attractor power. I admitted that even though my name and face are on the books and I have the microphone in my hand, I still desperately needed a spiritual kick in the ass. And that's why I'm so excited to write this book. Sitting here in my office, I already feel better. I feel empowered by the words that I know are coming, I'm energized by the pages

1

I've committed to write, and I feel ease just knowing that the answers are within me.

My excitement about this book is a massive statement to the Universe. It's my way of saying yes to feeling good, yes to healing my false perceptions, and yes to living with true freedom and joy. The Universe is always picking up what we're putting out. And today, I'm putting out an energy of joy for all that is to come from this miraculous writing journey ahead.

Right now, as I write this book, my spiritual cheerleader is coming through, and I'm so grateful. Because the past few months have been far from joyful. I got really out of alignment with the energy of joy and totally disconnected from my Super Attractor power. I was in the midst of launching my book *Judgment Detox*. Writing the book was a beautiful experience, but when it came time to launch it, I let myself get really stressed out. I was overwhelmed with thoughts of fear because I felt out of control, unsupported, and pressured to perform. I was in and out of manic manifesting, trying to force the Universe to give me the results I wanted. My work and personal relationships suffered due to my misalignment. And I had a lot of negative stories on repeat. The negative stories built up strong momentum, so much so that I got physically sick and depressed. Worst of all, I felt tremendous guilt because I was so disconnected from the true source of power on which I've grown to rely. Each negative thought, controlling action, and fear-based response continued to tell the Universe that I was a yes for chaos.

We become out of alignment when we get hooked into fear-based, low-energy thoughts. The metaphysical text *A Course in Miracles* teaches, "There are no 'idle' thoughts. All thinking produces form on some level." Each thought we have emits energy. That energy either brings us closer to the supportive flow of the Universe or resists it. The energy

2

behind our thoughts directly affects our experiences. When we have a fear-based, low-vibe thought on repeat, it creates energetic momentum that will eventually start to manifest in our lives. For instance, throughout the *Judgment Detox* book launch, I kept repeating the thought, "If I don't do it, no one else will." This is an old story for me. I replayed this thought over and over, and eventually it became my reality. I wound up controlling every detail and felt unsupported because I wouldn't let anyone support me. My thoughts of being unsupported became my experience.

I can tell when I'm out of alignment because I become focused on outside goals and objectives as opposed to the joy of life. When I'm misaligned, I try to control my circumstances. I'm resentful, my energy is low, and I feel physically ill. It's a struggle to get things done, and I cut off the flow of inspiration.

By contrast, when I'm in alignment with the Universe, I feel happy and excited regardless of what my circumstances may be. I'm hopeful and positive even when I face challenges. I'm not worried, stressed, or focused on problems. Good things flow to me, and I feel creativity moving through me. People want to support me, and I find a way through every block.

Two weeks before my book tour for *Judgment Detox* ended, it became clear to me that I was badly out of alignment. I hit bottom with my negative thoughts and patterns. It was like I was energetically strangling the book launch. I tried to control the process, became obsessed with the outcome, and let stress be the driving force behind every action I took. I was miserable and couldn't sustain that behavior, and I had no choice but to pivot. One night I said to my husband, "I'm done with the drama. I'm changing the story. I'm getting more help, and I'm clearing space to focus on my gifts. I want to write more, speak more, and live in my creative force. I welcome the Universe to support this shift now."

The words I spoke were more than just words. What I experienced was an energy shift. I accepted that in an instant I could choose again and redirect my life. I embraced the truth: The instant we realign with love, the Universe responds powerfully. In any given moment, we can change our story and say yes to what we truly want. As soon as we do, the Universe delivers.

Within seconds of saying my prayer, I started feeling better. And I let that good-feeling momentum carry me. I started dreaming about the people I'd hire to get me into a space where I could focus on my creative work. I committed to relaxing and restoring. Days later I headed to California to close out the tour, and I had the time of my life. The event planning went perfectly, the media helped get the word out, and the audience members had a blast. On stage, I allowed myself to surrender to my art and let the Universal creative force move through me. My husband noticed my shift and said, "All right, what happened? You're in such a better place." I said, "I told the Universe I was ready to realign."

The key to getting back into alignment is to want it. In an instant we can forgive our fear and choose again. We can start a new story, shift our perceptions, and allow miracles to unfold. Low-vibe thoughts become addictive, and as with any addiction, we need to interrupt the pattern to heal it. This book will offer powerful tools to help you interrupt negative energy and low-vibe thoughts so that you can redirect your life to flow toward what you desire—and most importantly, so that you can feel good, release control, and trust in the Universe.

Throughout the book I'll reference one of my favorite spiritual teachers, Abraham-Hicks, often known just as Abraham. Abraham is the work of a woman named Esther Hicks, who is a channel for lessons and teachings on the topic of the Law of Attraction. She is one of the most powerful practitioners in the field. "Abraham" is treated as a plural noun because the name represents a collective spiritual energy who have described themselves as "a group consciousness from the non-physical dimension." My own teachings and personal life have been greatly influenced by Abraham, and I'm proud to share their teachings throughout this book. Abraham-Hicks say, "There is only a stream of Well-Being that flows. You can allow it or resist it, but it flows just the same." The stream of well-being is an ever-present flow of love, creativity, inspiration, and peace. When our energy vibrates with love, we match the creative force of the Universe. When you're in this flow, you know that no matter your circumstances, there is a spiritual solution. You feel a sense of freedom and faith that what you desire is on the way even if you can't see it yet. You have more fun and you feel better. Invisible doors open for you, and creative opportunities present themselves without effort. You can do less and receive more. When you're in alignment with the flow of the Universe, you are a Super Attractor creating the life you want and attracting more than you could otherwise imagine simply by choosing to feel good. Life is much easier when you realign with the Universe.

So today I ask you this important question: Are you ready to realign with the Universe?

I know the answer is yes. But I want to check in further.

Is the answer, "Hell yes, Gabby, I'm ready"?

Or is it a, "Yes, but . . . "?

This is an important distinction because even slight resistance will block the flow.

If you feel resistant or hesitant in answering this question, here's the solution: let's call out your resistance right now. It's actually very likely that you're out of alignment with the feeling of joy in some way, so don't freak out! Just forgive yourself now. Say this prayer silently or out loud to yourself: *I forgive my past, I release the future, and I honor how*

I feel in the present. The moment you forgive your past, you clear space for the present, and an energetic shift occurs. And here's the really exciting thing: at this moment right now, you're perfectly on track. The Universe is always saying YES, even when it doesn't necessarily feel like it. The simple act of reading this book means that you're a yes for joy, abundance, wellness, romance, and anything else you could possibly desire. Opening this book is a massive statement to the Universe that you're willing to realign with a higher power and be a Super Attractor. So if there are a lot of issues in your life right now, start by thanking them. The issues in our lives offer us a choice: we can let them take over, or we can let them help us pivot toward grace. The methods in this book will help you pivot.

As soon as you pivot, you begin your new life! A new way of perceiving the world, yourself, your relationships, and your physical body. Your desire to feel better is all you need to pivot toward alignment. So, my friend, let the pivoting begin.

Even the toughest experiences offer you great wisdom and direction. Be grateful for what has caused you discomfort, because it reveals to you what you still need to heal. Take a moment to thank the situations in your life that don't feel good. Bless these issues so that you can set them free. Take a minute now to see the job loss as an opportunity to shift your career toward work that brings you joy. See the breakup as a chance to love yourself more. Be open to perceiving a physical condition as a chance to get closer to God. The moment we choose to perceive our pain as the catalyst for great healing and growth, we realign with the power of the Universe. This gratitude helps you get out of the feeling of being the victim and into a state of positivity.

You may be thinking, "If I'm grateful for this stuff, aren't I sending the message that I'm okay with it?" Actually, the opposite is true. When you let difficult situations dominate your life, you give them power and momentum. As soon as you choose to see the light in the dark corners, you redirect your power toward what you want. Hard or unpleasant situations offer you clarity about what you don't want, thereby helping you discover what you do want. This is the first step back into alignment.

Throughout my life, these simple shifts have helped me transform darkness into light. One of the most powerful examples for me occurred on October 2, 2005. This was the day I chose to put down alcohol and drugs and get sober. That shift not only saved my life but also would ultimately go on to save the lives of many people. I wrote about my recovery in my book *Spirit Junkie,* and that work inspired readers around the world to find their own path to recovery. My willingness to see my addiction as a teacher, forgive myself, and choose love has helped countless people.

If you're struggling with any kind of addiction, whether it's to a substance, a behavior, or even to fearful thoughts, know that in this moment you can choose again. Your choice to see love will help you to redirect your life. Become willing right now to forgive yourself for all that was and celebrate all that you will become.

I feel empowered when I am grateful for the tough stuff. I can see even traumatic events and addictions as learning devices rather than shameful dark periods. Every difficult situation in my life, no matter how hard it seemed at the time, has offered me grace on the other side. I've made a choice to grow through pain and find honor in all that I've been through. Choosing to see difficult times with grace has helped me move out of the feeling of being a victim and feel proud of myself for my willingness to grow.

Of course, the goal isn't to have to fall apart to realign. The goal is to make alignment a daily priority. Since we're at the beginning of this journey, you may find that misalignment seems to be your default setting. Don't sweat it. The moment you find yourself out of alignment, you can be grateful for the lesson and forgive yourself fast.

You don't have to fix your whole life to feel better now! In fact, you don't have to do much at all. Begin your shift into alignment with a method I call "Choose Again."

THE 3-STEP CHOOSE AGAIN METHOD

When you begin this practice, I recommend you document each step in your Super Attractor journal (visit the book resources page at GabbyBernstein.com/SuperAttractor). The more you practice this method, the more it will become second nature. In time you'll be able to quickly follow the method in your mind whenever you need it. For now, however, let your journal support your path.

Step 1: Notice the thought.

When you find yourself stuck in negativity or fear, consciously step back. You can do this by noticing that your thoughts and energy are out of alignment with joy. Ask yourself, "How do I feel right now?" Write down your answer in your journal.

Step 2: Forgive the thought.

Forgive yourself for being misaligned and celebrate your desire to shift. Thank your negative feelings and thoughts for showing you what you don't want and revealing what you do. Next to each negative thought that you document, write the words *Thank you for revealing to me what I don't want so that I can clarify what I do want.*

Step 3: Choose again.

Answer this question in your journal: "What is the best-feeling thought I can find right now?" Then ask the Universe to guide you toward that thought. In your journal, write down this prayer or say it to yourself: *Thank you, Universe, for guiding my thoughts toward good-feeling emotions.*

As you practice this step, remember that you are reaching for the next best feeling. You are not required to land on the ultimate solution. So, for instance, if you are struggling with finances, the thought "I'm going to be out of debt in one week!" is likely to create *more* misalignment because you probably wouldn't believe it. Instead, choose a thought that feels realistic and possible. For this step to work, you must believe in your next best thought. If there's any doubt, then your energy won't back up your prayer. (Keep in mind that the Universe always hears your prayers. But your energy must support those prayers in order for *you* to hear the guidance that the Universe then provides.)

Let's look together at how we might apply the three steps of the Choose Again Method: As before, imagine someone who is suffering from financial lack and uncertainty. Understandably, this person's dominant thoughts center around debt and the crippling fear of not being able to pay their bills. They've become obsessed with these fearful thoughts because the inner voice of fear (otherwise known as the ego) has convinced them that the more they think about it, the more they can control their circumstances. It is at this stage that we can start to apply the initial step of recognizing the negative thoughts. It's normal, of course, to think that obsessing over an issue is how we find solutions. But it actually has the opposite effect. The more your mentality tends toward fear and lack, the further away you are from allowing solutions to come into your consciousness. We bring energy to the object of our focus. That energy influences our emotional state, and it's our emotional state that is our point of attraction. Fear-minded thinking puts us out of alignment with positive energy. When we're out of alignment with positive energy, we're disconnected from the support of the Universe. The Universe has the capacity to bring forth creative solutions for earning, new ways of managing money, and other ideas that the fear-based logical mind cannot come up with. But we have to be in a receptive place to hear the answers.

The way out of that negative loop is through Step 2, forgiving the misaligned thoughts. Through forgiveness, we can release the past and accept that the present moment offers an opportunity for grace. Even a slight moment of presence is enough to redirect our energy and get positive momentum to help choose a better thought. Moving to Step 3, we think, "What is the best-feeling thought I can find right now?" A nice way to get there in this instance could be with a statement like "I'm open to creative possibilities for abundance." This statement becomes a prayer. By saying this kind of affirmation silently or out loud, we make a massive announcement to the Universe that we are ready to choose again. The very second we choose a loving thought, our emotions shift and our energy changes. This is realignment with the Universe.

The Choose Again Method may seem too simple at first. You may be wondering how you can just shift out of negative thoughts that may have plagued you for years. I assure you that choosing to shift your thoughts doesn't have to be difficult. It does not matter whether these negative thoughts have been with you for 2 weeks or 20 years. The simple choice to feel better is enough to put you on a path to what you desire. So use these three steps to help you redirect your energy and slow down the flow of negativity.

The simplicity of this method might tempt you to dismiss its value. Let me be very clear: we don't have time to dwell in our drama. Being committed to a spiritual path means that we're ready to wake up fast. We need to make feeling good our highest priority and do whatever it takes to be Super Attractors. Our commitment to living in alignment will help us stay sane in these times. No matter where you are in the world, you cannot hide from the negative energy of the daily news, political climate, and feelings of divisiveness. Even if you were able to ignore the world around you, perhaps by avoidance or escapism, you would do so at the expense of the greater good. You would deprive the world of your positive energy, which affects not just you but everyone you come into contact with.

I live among just a few hundred neighbors in a rural town. Even here, in the peace and quiet of the countryside, I'm not immune to the negative energy of the world. All I have to do is turn on the news or scroll through social media to feel assaulted by low vibrations. But instead of dragging me down, it offers me an opportunity to practice the Choose Again Method and strengthen my connection to the Universe. When we become aware of how external negative vibrations affect us, we can follow the three steps and pivot fast. The only way to come back into loving alignment is to become aware of how we detour. Throughout this book I will encourage you to return to the Choose Again Method to witness your misalignment and come back to love fast.

It's important to understand that this method is not designed for you to bypass your problems. It's designed to help you attract solutions. Remember, the best-feeling thought you can reach for may not be the ultimate solution, but it will guide you to feel better. Every better-feeling emotion offers you guidance toward the solutions you seek and the joyful truth of who you are. Use this practice to gently

11

guide your energy back into alignment with the Universe so that you can be an energetic match for healing and guidance. The more you make this method a habit, the better you'll feel. And the better you feel, the more easily you will attract the feelings and experiences you want in your life.

Each chapter in this book will offer you new methods to help you strengthen your connection to the Universe, direct your desires, and become a Super Attractor. Before you embark on the rest of the lessons, it's helpful to always start by choosing again. Each step in the Choose Again Method is crucial to your alignment and holds a promise. Let's review:

In Step 1 you recognize your misalignment. You can't change a bad habit without admitting that it's there. All spiritual practice must begin with awareness, so become conscious of your misalignment and thank your thoughts and feelings. You show gratitude for these thoughts and feelings because they reveal what you don't want and guide you toward what you truly desire.

Step 2 is to forgive yourself for being misaligned. If not, you'll hold on to the past and stay stuck in the negative pattern no matter how hard you try to pivot. Forgive yourself, your thoughts, and anything that led you to this point. Accept that even the most difficult experiences in your life have given you an opportunity to grow if you choose to. We can be the victim of the world we see, or we can choose to perceive difficult past experiences as a catalyst for change.

And finally, you get the option to choose again. By reaching toward the best-feeling thought you can access, you're instantly put into a new vibrational state. This new thought is a prayer. With it, you send a message to the Universe that you want to feel better. In this new vibration, the Universe responds by guiding you to your next right action. The next right action may come to you as a better-feeling thought, as a new idea, or as a desire to end a harmful pattern. In

October 2005, the moment I chose to release my addiction and get sober, the Universe instantly directed me to call a friend to help me get to a recovery meeting. As soon as I asked for help, the Universe delivered.

Remember that we can't hear intuitive guidance from the Universe until we're willing to ask for help. Receiving spiritual guidance requires that we become attuned to the energy of the Universe. Imagine you're constantly complaining about your job to a close friend. They try to offer you guidance, but your incessant negativity and fear block you from even hearing their words. You resist their guidance because you're so focused on what isn't working. Then, finally, when things get too tough and you can't handle it anymore, you break down. You call your friend and ask for help. They respond with profoundly clear direction, compassion, and guidance. You say, "This is exactly what I needed to hear." They reply, "It's what I've been saying all along." Their guidance was the same. The only difference was that you chose to hear it.

It's no different with your relationship to the Universe. The Universe is always conspiring to support you, guide you, and compassionately lead you toward the highest good. When you're focused on chaos and fear, or trying to control everything, you deflect this support and guidance. But the moment you surrender, the Universe is there to pick you up off the floor and show you the way.

But you don't need to wait till you feel desperate to surrender. You don't have to keep spiraling downward till you've hit bottom and you're lying on the floor. You can make choosing again (and choosing love) your habit. Surrendering should be the *first* thing you do, not your last-ditch effort. The Choose Again Method is your path to clearer communication with the Universe.

My intention is to help you get into constant contact with the Universe. I've found that in certain areas of my life it's been easy to receive Universal guidance, whereas in others I've resisted. The areas where there's resistance are the ones where my dominant thoughts are still aligned with fear. I've done a lot of therapy, sober recovery, trauma healing, and various other practices to reorganize these dominant beliefs. But nothing helps me more than surrendering them to the Universe for help. As soon as I allow the Universe to replace my fear-based beliefs with new perceptions, I receive a miracle. Our analytical minds want to resist this simplicity. We want to think that it will take decades of recovery to change our beliefs. But Abraham-Hicks say, "A belief is just a thought you keep thinking." When you choose a new thought, a shift will occur.

I want you to choose again—and do so quickly—and follow the Universal guidance that's always available to you. When you choose again, resolution is offered. This doesn't mean that further healing isn't required. The solution might still be several steps away. So even if the issue doesn't seem fully resolved now, you can trust that you're being guided in the right direction. You can trust that when you let the Universe lead you, you'll receive Good Orderly Direction (the Universal force of love, also known as G-O-D). You will be given intuitive ideas of where to go and what to say. And you'll be more easily led to a way through every block.

When we choose again, we send a prayer to the Universe that we're ready to feel good. Back when I got sober, my mentor in recovery told me to get on my knees and ask God to help me stay clean. She said that when I felt the urge to relapse, I should never take matters into my own hands. She called that behavior "white-knuckling it." Instead, she suggested that I turn my addiction over to a higher power to help guide me back. At the time I didn't have much of a relationship with God or the Universe. I identified as a spiritual person, but I hadn't yet established what the concept of a higher power meant to me. Nonetheless, I followed her direction. She said, "Act as if and you will be led." So I got on my knees and started to pray daily. At the time my prayer was to stay clean and sober. Whenever I was tempted to pick up a drink or do a drug, I'd hit my knees and pray. At dinner parties and on dates, if I felt tempted, I'd excuse myself and go to the bathroom to pray and get centered. Prayer became my immediate response to any inner turmoil or addictive pull. Prayer became a habit. To this day, when I find myself out of alignment with peace, it's a sign that I've been relying on my own strength instead of the strength of a higher power. In those moments I follow the Choose Again Method: notice the thought, forgive the thought, choose again.

Praying doesn't have to mean kneeling beside your bed and talking to God. A prayer can come through a simple surrendered thought, when you decide that your will is no longer working and you invite in a higher power to take the lead. The instant you choose to think a better thought, you've asked to realign with a higher power. You can call it the Universe, call it angels, call it spirit, call it your inner guide, call it God. I don't care; just call on it. The methods in this book are backed with a prayer. They are designed to help you offer up your grievances and fears to a higher power. Surrender to each practice in this book, and strengthen your faith in the Universal energy of love. With your faith you'll feel safe and certain no matter what. Follow these methods to realign with the Universe and dissolve feelings of separation and doubt. My late mentor and friend Dr. Wayne Dyer said, "When you eliminate the concept of separation from your thoughts and your behavior, you begin to feel your connection to everything and everyone." That connection is your Super Attractor power.

You just have to clear the blocks to its presence. Each practice in this book will offer you a gradual opening to the energy that is available to you at all times. *Gradual* is the operative word. I don't expect you to shift from lack to abundance or sickness to health instantly. What I hope is that you follow these steps and gradually shift your perceptions, thoughts, and energy one moment at a time. This gradual effect will offer you long-lasting change. When you change your mind about your experience, your experience will change. This is a subtle but very potent shift that occurs when you pivot from darkness to light.

Keep it simple, follow my guidance, and let good-feeling emotions gently lead you back into alignment with your true nature!

Each method in this book will help get you back into alignment. My hope is that once you learn them, you'll use them interchangeably and make them part of your daily routine. The more you apply these methods in your life, the faster they will become second nature. We need practices for feeling good in order to make feeling good a habit. We've given more faith and energy to the negativity in our minds, and it's time to redirect our focus. By practicing these methods, you will be able to quickly shift from fear to joy and realign with your Super Attractor nature. Have fun with these tools and use them as often as possible!

There's no right or wrong way to apply these methods. Just make sure you're having fun! Don't let your spiritual practice become a chore. Let it be a reprieve from the world's drama and your inner turmoil. I've kept these methods simple so that you can do them easily and in the moment, no matter what you have going on in your life. These tools will catapult you back to your true, joyful nature. Aligning with the Universe must be a conscious choice we make all throughout the day.

BEGIN YOUR DAY IN ALIGNMENT

When we open our eyes in the morning, we can go in one of two directions: we can align with the Universe through spiritual practice, meditation, prayer, affirmation, or exercise . . . or we can pick up our phones, turn to the news, gulp down a cup of coffee, and start rushing around.

When we choose the second option, we often begin our day with negative vibrations and overwhelm. So it's imperative that we change our morning habits. The morning is a sacred time and must be cherished. It's when we choose how we want the rest of the day to go. A single shift in our behavior can redirect our entire day.

Set yourself up to win by starting your day with a practice that will get you aligned as soon as you wake up! I've found that this is the optimal time for aligning your energy with love. You've spent the night sleeping in an energy of nonresistance. Abraham-Hicks teach that when we sleep, we release resistance to negative thoughts. That means that when we wake up, we have a clean slate in front of us—an opportunity to release the negativity from the day before and begin again. That's why the first moments of the morning are so precious. We can take advantage of being in a state of nonresistance and start the day with a fresh attitude. Follow a morning practice to start your day in alignment and sustain your good-feeling emotions throughout the day.

I've built up a wealth of spiritual practices to turn to as soon as I wake up. I created the Spirit Junkie App, which is set to show me a positive affirmation first thing (you can find the app at GabbyBernstein.com/SuperAttractor). Then I set my phone to airplane mode and meditate. But there's one morning practice in particular that has changed my life: once I've gotten out of bed and brushed my teeth, I recite positive mantras! The mantras guide me to return to the love of the Universe, accept myself, and forgive myself for any misalignment from the day before. I affirm how I want to feel, who I want to be, and how I want to show up in the world. I affirm self-love and compassion. I affirm my willingness to feel good. This practice has been a saving grace for me. It instantly puts me into spiritual, physical, and emotional alignment. Affirming positivity helps me take advantage of my connection to the Universe and ride that positive momentum throughout the day.

The moment you wake up, you can recite the following mantras silently or out loud. Or you can download my audio mantras that are backed with inspirational music at GabbyBernstein.com/SuperAttractor. You can use them first thing in the morning and even throughout the day. Regardless of how you feel when you wake up in the morning, these affirmations will help you get into alignment. These words can greatly support you even when you don't believe in them. Just say them out loud and let the power of your intentions get you back into alignment. I've made this practice a daily routine, and I hope it brings you as much joy as it has brought me.

YOUR MORNING MANTRAS

My body is rested and my mind is clear.

I start my day with positive thoughts and energy.

I am relaxed, nonresistant, and clear.

My day unfolds with ease and grace.

People support me throughout the day.

The Universe supports my desires today.

I am open to receiving greatness.

I am energized and inspired.

Creative possibilities are available to me.

Nothing holds me back.

I take action with faith and clarity.

I am healthy, well, and vibrant.

Today is a great day.

I'm having fun today.

I bring joy to others.

I bring light with me wherever I go.

I am a positive influence on the world.

All is well.

Repeating these mantras on your own or with the audio download will immediately shift you into an empowered energy and positive vibration. I invite you to make this method part of your daily routine. It will help you clear mental blocks, release resistance, and set yourself up for a miraculous day. Spending even five minutes in affirmation is enough to change the direction of your day.

If you have kids, get them in on this practice too! Imagine how empowered a child would feel if they started their day with positivity. There's no greater practice to set your kid up to feel great.

By applying the Choose Again Method and mantras, you will begin to feel better. But the moment you start feeling good, it's possible something sneaky may happen. Your ego (the inner voice of fear) will resist your good feelings. The ego's voice has been your dominant inner dialogue for so long that it may have a stronghold on your subconscious. That's okay, though, because we're calling it out in the next chapter! In Chapter 2 I will help you become aware of the ways that the ego will resist feeling good. I'll help you accept that it's good to feel good. Positive-feeling emotions are our birthright, and in this next chapter you'll become unapologetic about how you want to feel. Don't be afraid of the ego, because your commitment to love is stronger than fear. And I've got your back every step of the way.

Chapter 2

IT'S GOOD TO FEEL GOOD

Of all the blocks to our Super Attractor power, the biggest is our resistance to feeling good. Don't believe me? Ask yourself: Have you come to rely on fear as a form of protection against feeling disappointment or hurt? It becomes so easy to slip into this way of thinking that you may not even be aware of it. Fear can feel like a natural way to protect yourself and stay in control. We've all come to be far more comfortable in a state of fear than in a place of joy and faith. You may be thinking, "Wait, I don't walk around feeling scared all the time. How am I relying on fear?" The answer is that fear takes many forms, and emotions you likely recognize—such as anxiety, defensiveness, judgment, and the impulse to control—really stem from a sense of fear. Think of fear as the opposite of love. When you rely on fear, as most of us do, you are disconnected from the free-flowing love of the Universe.

The unfortunate truth is, many of us are addicted to fear. We've become so accustomed to the fearful projections of the world that we don't trust that things can be good. Unconsciously we think that if we focus on the good stuff, we will lose control, be unsafe, or be susceptible to disappointment. The ego has convinced us that "good" is limited and eventually our luck will run out. We suspect that anything really good is probably too good to be true. Society has convinced us that if something is worth having, it requires struggle, heroic perseverance, and sacrifice. Therefore, we've become addicted to suffering, and this mind-set actually increases our struggling! When we believe we need to suffer, we tell the Universe it's what we want. Remember the message of Chapter 1: the Universe always delivers. If we believe in suffering, we will suffer.

What I'm about to say may startle you. I want you to read this next sentence as many times as you need to in order for it to sink in:

**In order to truly live as a Super Attractor,
we must accept that good things can come easily.**

This is likely the opposite of everything you've ever been taught! This is because most of us have it all backward. For our whole lives, we've held on to fear-based belief systems to feel safe. We believe in thoughts like "I have to work incredibly hard to succeed," "I'm too old to have a baby," and "I'm terrible at relationships." Can you see how all these thoughts are backed with an energy of resistance? Our resistance to feeling good is what blocks the good that we want to attract. The moment we release that resistance and let ourselves feel good, then everything we truly desire begins to come to us naturally. When we feel good, we attract solutions rather than problems. When we feel good, life flows naturally.

I know it's hard to get your head around this. Many students of spiritual practices (including me) believe this concept but have a difficult time applying it. Fear has a strong hold on us. We resist feeling good so much that we expect life to be hard.

By way of example, here is how fear presented itself in the early part of my career. In the first decade of building my business, I experienced a lot of joy and faith. But beneath that joy and faith was an ever-present undercurrent of fear. I was scared that if I weren't working my ass off, then my career would all fall apart. This belief system stemmed from childhood. When I was young, I picked up the story that "If I don't do it, no one else will." I spent my life believing that I had to strive hard and overwork in order to get what I wanted. My career continued to move forward because the joy and faith were stronger than the fear. But even though I was having fun and achieving success, I always felt as if it had to be hard or it wouldn't continue to work. No matter how inspired I felt or what I accomplished, I always felt as if I was fighting, and that there was *always* more to do. The belief "If I don't do it, no one else will" was blocking my Super Attractor power. And even though the Universe presented me with a lot of opportunity and success, it didn't come without struggle. I knew deep down that there had to be a better way, but for a long time I wasn't ready to truly access it.

It wasn't until 2016 that I hit bottom with my workaholism. My struggling and stress finally took me down. My belief that I had to do it all created a world where I felt very unsupported, fearful, and alone. My body was falling apart, I was barely holding my business together, and my relationships were suffering. Then I hit bottom. Often, a bottom is a moment of surrender, and in this case it was for me. In this surrendered state, I said the words out loud: "There has to be a better way." I could no longer resist help from others, and most of all I couldn't continue to resist support from the Universe. Once I hit this bottom, I received a gift. I could finally see how I was terrified of feeling good. I realized that I equated feeling good with losing control. Worst of all, I was afraid of surrendering to the higher power of the Universe. I believed that I had to rely on myself and that I had to suffer to succeed. While this belief system was deeply ingrained in my psyche, the Universe had begun to present a spiritual solution.

The moment I hit my knees and surrendered to the Universe, clear direction was presented to me. As soon as I became willing to change my belief that I was unsupported, support came through! It first showed up as intuition. When we realign with the Universe, we can receive loving direction as an inner knowing. Sometimes it can come as a hit of inspiration or a download of information. This time I heard very clear intuitive direction. I was journaling one morning and my hand started to move faster than usual. My handwriting shifted and the words on the page took on a different tone. I knew that I was receiving direction from a Universal presence. These words came onto the page: *Pay attention to the places where you feel supported. Feel the feelings of support, and continue to feel them more.*

I was so moved by this spiritual guidance that I put it into practice right away. I asked myself, "Where do I feel supported?" Instantly a thought came into my mind about my event planner, Anette. The only area in my career where I'd ever allowed anyone to support me was in putting together events. For several years I'd collaborated with Anette to plan my book tours and large-scale events. Anette is a powerhouse who gets the job done! She is so confident and in charge, and her energy takes over in such a way that you have no choice but to surrender to her support. No matter how hard I'd try to control things, Anette would always remind me to get out of the way and trust her. When I was working with Anette, I always had faith that everything was fully taken care of. I felt greatly supported and at ease. I knew Anette had my back.

I started to put this feeling of support into action. After journaling and receiving this intuitive hit, I spent several minutes daydreaming about how much I loved Anette and how supported she made me feel. Then I wrote in my journal, "When I'm working with Anette, I feel like everything is happening around me and I'm truly taken care of." Let me tell you, it *felt so great* to write down these words. This statement affirmed exactly how good I wanted to feel! And it felt so good to feel good. The Universal direction I'd received in my journal was exactly what I needed to redirect my energy and put me back into alignment with the support of the Universe.

I repeated this for months: "Everything is happening around me and I'm truly taken care of." I said it while driving, while cooking, before I went to bed, and when I woke up in the morning. It became my mantra. In those moments when I felt the urge to take over anything, from a big project to a small task, and do everything myself, I turned to this mantra.

Not only did I repeat this mantra all day, I also spent my stillness practice meditating on the feeling of what it was like to work with Anette. I'd see myself backstage, feeling totally relaxed knowing that she was handling everything. I'd envision myself walking onto the stage, seeing everyone happily settled in their seats, and feeling free knowing that all the important elements and countless little details alike were handled. Over the next few months, I spent hours in meditation feeling this feeling and re-creating the experience of being supported by Anette. I put energy, visions, and enthusiasm into this feeling. I reveled in it. I surrendered to feeling good!

Within months of starting this practice, I started to notice things dramatically change in my business. Without even realizing it, I'd attracted two new people to help.

I was finally letting my husband own his role, and I was delegating my responsibilities left and right. In a few short months, I started to get out of the way and let others in. This was a miracle! Feeling good guided me toward what I truly wanted. I could finally focus on being an empowering spiritual teacher—and more importantly, I could release the fear of not being supported and the belief that I had to do everything myself.

THE KEY TO FEELING GOOD IS TO DECIDE TO STOP FEELING BAD

In order to feel good, you must decide to stop feeling bad. It's as simple and profound as that. There is no other way. For far too long, we have resisted this decision because we've been waiting for our life's circumstances to give us a *reason* to feel good. In fact, many of us don't even realize that feeling bad is a decision we've made. We think things like "I'll feel good when I get a clean bill of health" or "I'll feel good when I have the money in the bank." When we do this, we're putting the outcome before the feeling. We have it all twisted! We think that we must live in fear in order to get something we want, which will then allow us to feel good. But the truth is that once you feel good, you start to easily attract what you desire! When we make feeling good our priority, everything else can flow.

A lot of people get hung up on the limiting belief that they're not worthy of feeling good and having what they want. Struggle becomes a habit, and joy is an afterthought. I'm asking you to see things totally differently. If you think you're not worthy of feeling good, then you're out of alignment with the truth of who you are. The loving energy of the Universe, the magnificence of God, the serenity of spirit is all within us. There is not a source outside of us that can save us from our sense of unworthiness. When we truly accept that we embody the power of love, then we can start to realign with the belief that we are worthy of feeling good. Feeling good is feeling God. By that I mean that when we feel good, we remember the God within us. Accepting our greatness is the key to being a Super Attractor. Let these methods help you stand in certainty that you are good and that, when you embody this truth, good things flow to you naturally.

Feeling good is good for its own sake! I learned this from Deepak Chopra at an event I was co-hosting with him and Eckhart Tolle in 2016. In between my hosting duties, I stood backstage listening to Deepak and Eckhart speak about their spiritual beliefs. At one point Deepak said that when you're happy for a particular *reason*, you're still in misery—because that reason can be taken from you tomorrow. His words reminded me that when we focus on what we think we need, we weaken our faith in the Universe.

Deciding to feel good is easier than you think! The Universe has been patiently awaiting your decision to feel good, and this decision is especially needed in your darkest moments. The Universe is guiding us even when we resist it. The instant we release our resistance, a flood of support and love rushes in. It's important to accept this. This isn't a "fake it till you make it" exercise. *The Universe wants you to feel good and wants to guide you toward exactly what you want and need.* Remember, you are one with the Universal energy of love, and feeling good is your birthright.

Don't just take my word for it! Let me help you see the Universe in action. Take any area of your life where you're struggling and want to feel better. Fill in the blank in the sentence below:

I recognize I'm out of alignment with [name a person, situation, belief system, etc.]. I choose to release the outcome and feel good now. Thank you, Universe, for guiding me.

This statement is a prayer. You're humbly offering your fear over to the Universe, and you are claiming your desire to feel good! We can't wait for our circumstances to change to feel good. The more good-feeling emotions you bring to your current circumstances, the faster things begin to work out the way you want, and the faster you feel better.

THINK IT TO FEEL IT METHOD

The Think It to Feel It Method lets you borrow a moment of happiness that you're able to identify and apply it to a situation where you're otherwise struggling. To get started, conjure up an area of your life where your desired emotion has shown up. It could be in a situation from your past or even an image you have of your future self. You can also think of someone in your life who displays that characteristic you would like for yourself.

Let me give you an example that illustrates this method. For me, one of my big desires, and an area where I struggle, is to be more relaxed even when things aren't going as planned. I don't have many experiences from my own life where I've been calm in the midst of something going wrong, so it's hard to bring one to mind and call on that feeling from my own memory. But when I think about how I might want to feel, I am instantly reminded of my friend Elisa. Her attitude is relaxed and calm even in the most chaotic of circumstances. I can envision her saying, "Okay, everything's working out." She can turn to that place of certainty no matter what's happening around her. I love this about her, and I want to embody it for myself. So even though I can't find that quality in myself yet, I know what it looks like and feels like to be around someone who has it. Elisa represents an attitude I can creatively call on as my desired feeling.

The most important part of this method is that the circumstances you choose to focus on *make you feel good*! If thinking about your first boyfriend makes you feel the romance you want to experience in your life today, then think it to feel it! If thinking about a time when you loved your job makes you feel confident and happy, then think it to feel it! It's safe to recall good memories or experiences. It's safe to look to others to reflect back to us what we want. We aren't comparing, but instead finding a good-feeling emotion in a situation where feeling good is difficult for us. We often think that if we had something in the past, we can't have it again. We may be scared to dwell in those good feelings for fear that we'll long for what once was. Similarly, we avoid thinking too much about other people's abundance and happiness. We think there's not enough to go around and that another person's success in some way indicates our failure. The opposite is true. All these experiences mirror to us a part of who we are. They mirror our desire for that feeling. And all manifestation begins with desire.

AFFIRM HOW YOU WANT TO FEEL

Now that you have a clearer idea of how you want to feel, you're ready to put it into action in your everyday life!

Affirm in your journal how you want to feel. Remember my affirmation, "Everything is happening around me, and I'm truly taken care of." Those words made me feel so good. Your affirmation should make you feel *good*. Be unapologetic about how you want to feel, and affirm it now!

Write your affirmation in your journal.

Now let's check in with how your affirmation makes you feel. On a scale of 0 to 10 (10 being the best feeling), where does this affirmation fall? If you're under a 7, then I recommend you rewrite your affirmation in a simpler way.

You must believe in your affirmation for it to take effect. For instance, if you're struggling with your body image, and your affirmation is "I love everything about my body," there might be a disconnect. Right now your energy is so focused on disliking (or even hating) your body that it's tough to reach for body love. Instead, you could affirm something that feels closer to what you believe in. Something like "I respect my body" or "I'm willing to start loving my body." The key is to believe in the affirmation even if it hasn't come into form yet. I believed in my affirmation even when it was only Anette who reflected it back to me. The words felt good to me, and that's how I knew I could use the statement to help me proactively co-create a new reality.

If you were under a 7 on the 0–10 scale, rewrite your affirmation in your journal so that you believe in it and it makes you feel great.

Once you've confirmed your affirmation, it's time to start using it. Set it as an alarm on your phone, or make it your phone's lock screen. Write it on a sticky note and put it on your computer, fridge, mirror, or car dashboard. Recite it morning, noon, and night. Whenever you notice yourself falling back into negative thoughts, repeat your affirmation a few times in a row to replace the low-vibe momentum. This is a powerful action! Your affirmation can slow down the negative momentum in your mind and allow you to quickly align with how you truly want to feel.

The Think It to Feel It Method, like every other method in this book, is designed to raise your vibration. Commit to your affirmation and take it seriously. Turn to it regularly. If you tend to forget or easily fall back into old patterns, then make sure to follow my tips above and reinforce your affirmation with phone alarms, sticky notes, and other visible reminders. Make it a habit and you will soon see just how powerful it is.

FEEL THE FEELINGS

The next step in assuming the energy of how you want to feel is to relish feeling good! Devote 10 minutes a day to sitting in meditation and allowing yourself to feel the feelings of your affirmation. If you are new to meditation, get excited! This is a practice even complete beginners can do easily. All you need is a quiet, comfortable place to sit. Just be sure you're relaxed and sitting in a straight but natural posture. This meditation practice begins with a journaling exercise, so have your journal by your side.

Once you're seated comfortably, open your journal and write your new "feel-good" affirmation at the top of the page. Then, for a few minutes, write about how this desire makes you feel. Write only about the positive aspects of this desire. Direct your writing toward ideas and visions that make you feel good. If any other thought or idea comes to mind, swiftly reach for a better feeling and write it down. Proactively guide yourself to a positive vision of your desire. When you're done writing, take a moment to read over what you put onto the page. Let your words inspire you and ignite good-feeling emotions.

Now it's time to meditate on these positive feelings. Gently close your eyes and breathe into the high-vibe feelings that you've cultivated through this writing exercise. Breathe long and deep. With every inhale, feel more deeply into the positive feeling.

Sit as long as you want to, and allow the good-feeling emotions to take over your psyche. If you have a negative thought, just gently replace it with your affirmation.

If visualizing yourself into your desired feelings seems difficult, you can instead sit for 10 minutes and silently repeat your affirmation. Let your positive affirmation replace any negative thoughts you may have. If you want my support

with this contemplative practice, visit GabbyBernstein.com/
SuperAttractor and download my guided meditation and
suggested music.

This meditation is an exercise in assuming the energy of
how you want to feel. Remember, the Universe responds to
your energy! Being a Super Attractor requires that we align
with the energy of what we want to attract. This step is crucial in the process of alignment. When you're happy for no
particular reason, you become a magnet for what you desire!
When you loosen your grip on the outcome and focus on
feeling good, good things come to you naturally. You're no
longer relying on getting something or somewhere to feel
good. You just feel good and allow. I strongly recommend
you make this a daily practice so that you keep the high-vibe
momentum moving in the direction of what you're ready
to receive.

ALLOW THE FLOW OF UNIVERSAL GUIDANCE

As soon as you start repeating your affirmation and
focusing on feeling good, you'll begin to notice the Universe
supporting you. In an instant the Universe can sweep in and
rearrange your perspective. The moment you surrender your
fear to the Universe, love takes over. Your only job now is to
let love come through. Welcome and trust in every single
feeling of support and every moment of synchronicity. The
more you embrace the wonder of Universal guidance, the
more it will show up in your life. What you believe, you will
perceive. Choose to focus on the guidance, intuition, and
direction that comes through. Whenever I affirm good-feeling
thoughts and emotions, the Universe positively redirects my
day! I'm given creative possibilities for problems I otherwise
could not solve. I receive intuitions about how to handle

situations that once overwhelmed me. I feel a sense of peace and faith. Feeling good aligns us with the Universe. This alignment offers us health, mental clarity, confidence, and reduced stress and anxiety. When we feel good, we are the opposite of resistant. We are receptive.

MAKE FEELING GOOD A PRACTICE

In order to feel good consistently, we have to make it a practice. It's likely you're used to waiting for your outside circumstances to dictate how you feel. This whole book is a process of unlearning that habit! I want to help you learn how to access good-feeling emotions even when things aren't working out as you planned. Dedicate time each day to consciously focus on feeling good so that in time it becomes your default state.

In addition to repeating your affirmation and meditating on good feelings, I suggest you do more things that make you happy. That's right—I am giving you permission to make having fun your top priority! This doesn't mean you have to quit your job and go live on a beach. Instead, think about all the activities in your daily life that make you happy. Identify the things you do that bring you joy, and do them more often.

Make feeling good a priority the same way you might make exercise or family a priority. If this is totally new to you or you suspect you'll revert to old habits in a few days, I suggest scheduling these activities into your calendar as you would a meeting! This isn't about turning fun into another obligation; it's about making it a priority. If you know you need some structure in order to honor this priority, that's okay! In time it will become a habit. Remember to be deliberate and bring conscious awareness to feeling good.

To be frank, we typically put everything else before feeling good. Most of us don't necessarily think much about this. Or we might even think it's virtuous. (If you've ever felt a hit of self-righteous satisfaction for being busier and more stressed-out than your friends or co-workers, you know this feeling!) But here is the truth: when we put everything else before feeling good, we're putting those things before our connection to our Super Attractor power. Whatever we put before our spiritual connection will suffer greatly. You may achieve what you want, but you *will* struggle and feel like crap all along the way. This is a whole new way of being. Feeling good must come first. Everything else will follow.

You now have several methods for aligning with good-feeling emotions:

- You can call on your affirmation to shift your thoughts.
- You can sit in your meditation to shift your energy.
- You can do something that brings you joy to realign with the Universe.

Use these methods to make feeling good your highest priority!

I want to emphasize an important point: you shouldn't be afraid to feel good when things aren't working out. When things don't go our way, our immediate reaction is to dwell in negativity. We can't even imagine feeling good in the midst of something going wrong. But feeling good is the quickest way out of what is wrong. Try it for yourself the next time something doesn't go your way. Do something to feel good fast. Listen to your favorite guided meditation. Call a friend who always makes you laugh. Take a walk outside. Allow yourself to access happiness even in the midst of a difficult time. That joy will be your guide out of the negative experience. It's totally fine to let yourself feel discomfort, but don't be afraid to balance it with joy. The good-feeling emotions will realign you with the Universe, and the Universe will be your guide. Make feeling good a priority, and you will be guided.

GIVE YOURSELF PERMISSION TO FEEL GOOD

It's easy to deny yourself good-feeling emotions. Maybe my story of overworking resonates with you, and you're sure that success requires struggle. Maybe you think the only way to be safe and secure is to control everything. Maybe you feel defeated by the dating scene. Or maybe you simply don't believe that you're worthy of feeling good. I have a lot of compassion for wherever you are at this point. The world we've grown to rely on has taught us to struggle. Every day we're inundated with bad news, reasons to compare ourselves to others, and a pervasive focus on the negative. Many of us have internal sources of struggle as well, such as health conditions and past traumas, that can get in the way of feeling good.

But now is the time to change that pattern. Loosen your grip on life, let yourself be free in these practices, and don't judge yourself for releasing control. Giving yourself permission to feel good is a perceptual shift. It may take practice and repetition, but when you commit to feeling good, your life will change in miraculous ways. You may have to remind yourself regularly that it's okay to feel good. Even now, as I write this book, I'm in the process of giving myself permission to slow down and take better care of myself even if it means saying no to personal or business opportunities. My intention is to feel good first before I do anything else.

And if that means I have to say no, then I will. This new pattern is uncomfortable for me because I've spent decades overworking and overachieving. But with each day that goes by, I feel more and more comfortable with my new normal. I'm beginning to accept that the less I do, the more I will succeed—because the less I do, the better I feel, and I bring that good feeling to the projects that I do take on. Sometimes I catch myself wanting to revert to old behavior, but it won't take me out of the flow. In those moments I return to my affirmation. My commitment to feeling good is stronger than the pull of my old patterns. The more time I devote to feeling good, the easier my life becomes. Each day I continue to give myself permission to feel good above all else, and the payoff is miraculous! I feel supported, I have the time and mental space to be creative, and my family and business are thriving.

WATCH YOUR WORDS AND THE WORDS OF OTHERS

It's very important to recognize the power of your words. Simple words can direct you on the right path or lead you down a fear-based spiral that brings you into a state of misalignment. For example, around the time that I was writing this book, things had gotten very hectic in my business. We were growing rapidly and desperately needed to hire more people. My team was super on top of everything, but they were feeling overwhelmed. Without realizing it, the company mantra had become "We have so much going on and we can't keep up with it!" This mantra started with me. On every call I'd worry that everyone was too busy, or we would talk about how much we had to get done. My words started to infiltrate the team. Within weeks all I kept hearing everyone say was "I just don't have time to get it all done. I'm so overwhelmed." Then I started to notice how their resistance was making me feel out of alignment with the good vibes I'm used to exuding. It was resulting in low energy, a negative mantra, and low morale. Then one afternoon, while working on this chapter, I had a major aha moment. I was at this exact point in the chapter, where I'm writing about the vibration of words, and I screamed, "Yikes, I'm not doing this!" Within minutes I scheduled a team call and got everyone on the videoconference line. I explained how my urgency and words were bringing them down and gently showed them how they had picked up what I was putting out. I asked us all to change the dialogue about what was happening. I practiced the Choose Again Method in real time and started to reach for good-feeling thoughts. I said things like "We are blessed. We have a message that is spreading rapidly, and we're growing fast. This is such an awesome position to be in. I'm confident in our ability to attract additional support. We're doing our passion work, and we're fulfilled every day. The Universe is expanding time for us when we choose to have fun along the way." Right after this redirect, I noticed the energy of the team shift. Their eyes lit up, they had huge smiles on their faces, and I could sense their relief. We'd chosen the wrong words to describe our circumstances, and we were all ready to choose again! With our new language, we began moving forward with power, enthusiasm, and a Super Attractor energy.

As this story shows, it's important to become conscious of how your words affect other people. When you gossip, complain, judge, or put others down, you weaken your vibrational alignment with the Universe. Be conscious of your words even when you think what you're saying is helpful, because the language you use can be damaging.

When you're fine-tuning your Super Attractor connection, it's also important to protect your own energy from other people's words. For instance, while I was going through my fertility journey, I was very open publicly about my personal experience of trying to conceive. In my book *The Universe Has Your Back*, I wrote about how my fertility journey was my greatest teacher in surrender. I knew my openness was helping women who were going through the same thing. I felt empowered by writing and speaking publicly about my experience. Sharing in this way opened the floodgates for many women to tell me their stories. I received emails, texts, and social media messages from women all over the world wanting to share their miracles and their struggles. While I felt very grateful for their outreach, I also noticed myself feeling down. Several women emailed me their stories of hardship and heartache. Over the years of being a spiritual teacher, I have welcomed people's stories and held each one with deep compassion. But this time it was too close to home. I began to feel my faith dwindle and my positive momentum slow down. I started to worry about some of the stories I was hearing and project them onto myself. I became very conscious of how other people's words were affecting me. So as soon as I noticed that I wasn't feeling good, I decided to pivot. I began to change the way I interpreted this information. When someone shared a negative fertility story with me, I'd immediately help guide them to a better place. Or if I received an email that suggested resistance around fertility, I'd say a prayer for the person and gently remind myself that their story wasn't mine. I did everything I could to protect my good-feeling momentum.

After several months of gently deflecting the negative stories and choosing to commit to feeling good, something interesting happened. I noticed that I was no longer getting negative messages or comments at all. It was almost as if I was immune to them. My commitment to feeling good sent out a message to the Universe that I was no longer a match for negative fertility stories. Not only was I no longer hearing the negative stories, but I was also attracting so many happy stories. Every woman I heard from was coming to me with positive, miraculous stories of fertility. It was amazing to see how my commitment to feeling good made me a Super Attractor for stories that would support my intention.

As you begin the practice of feeling good, you will notice a lot of resistance from the outside world. Don't blame others for their resistance. They're merely reflecting back to you any lingering resistance of your own. Use these moments as opportunities to surrender to feeling good. You can't control what people say or do, but you can control how you choose to perceive it. Practice protecting your good-feeling emotions at all costs. Darkness cannot coexist in your light, so keep shining! In certain settings, you may need to redirect conversations, unfollow people on social media, or even leave the room. Be kind and loving toward others while creating clear boundaries that protect your good-feeling emotions. You can choose how you perceive your world. You are the dreamer of your dream.

DON'T SABOTAGE THE GOOD-FEELING FLOW

Throughout my career I've met thousands of people who have transformed their lives by adopting a spiritual practice. They share stories about how, as soon as they changed their thoughts and energy, they began to attract what they wanted into their lives. As they shifted their point of attraction, they became Super Attractors for what they truly desired. However, many of the same people told me that as soon as they started to feel better and began to attract what they wanted, out of nowhere, a fearful voice began to question, "Is this too good to be true?" The voice of fear started to sabotage their good-feeling emotions. Their faith in fear took over, and they fell back into the old pattern of negative thoughts and fear-based attracting.

I want to call this out now so that you're constantly checking in with yourself. If you apply each method in this book, you will begin to feel miraculous shifts and experience mind-blowing results. This is not an exaggeration. The second you align yourself with good-feeling emotions, your Super Attractor power begins to set in. But as quickly as your power turns on, fear can show up to block it. So let's call it out now. Your fear is going to do anything it can to sabotage your Super Attractor mojo. But don't fear your fear. Just be aware of it. When fear tries to take you out of alignment, return to your Choose Again Method from Chapter 1 to stay in the good-feeling flow.

Here's how you can use the Choose Again Method when you notice fear sabotaging your flow:

1. Notice the fear.

Notice when your fearful thoughts start sabotaging your positive flow, and ask yourself, "How do I feel right now?" Let yourself feel whatever is coming up for you.

2. Forgive the thought.

Forgive yourself for fearing the good feelings. Say out loud or silently, "I forgive this thought, and I choose to believe in love instead." Then celebrate your desire to shift back to feeling good!

3. Choose again.

Answer this question: "What is the best-feeling thought I can find right now?" Then thank the Universe for guiding you toward that thought.

Use your Choose Again Method to come back fast and say no to self-sabotage. Becoming a Super Attractor will require you to repeat new positive behavior regularly. Now is your time to make feeling good a habit! (There's more of this waiting for you. In the coming chapters, I'll give you a really powerful method for thinking your way into feeling better.)

BE SATISFIED WITH WHAT IS

You may find great relief in these methods and notice immediate changes. But there might also be some areas of your life that take a bit longer to shift. That's totally fine. The goal isn't to change everything about your life over-night. The goal is to have fun along the way to what you desire! Abraham-Hicks say:

The reason you want every single thing that you want, is because you think you will feel really good when you get there. But if you don't feel really good on your way to there, you can't get there. You have to be satisfied with what-is while you're reaching for more.

Your satisfaction with what is allows you to be happy and peaceful regardless of whether you have exactly what you think you need. So just forget what you think you need and focus on feeling good! Feeling good will bring you far more than whatever you thought you needed. You'll release the need to get something, be somewhere, or have certain circumstances in place to be happy. Happiness will become the outcome you desire most.

Commit to the practices in this chapter. They will pre-pare you for the manifesting to come, because in order to attract all that's good, you must first believe you are worthy of feeling good. The methods you've learned so far will help you welcome worthiness and happiness and prepare you to *claim* all that you will attract.

Enjoy the practice of feeling good. As I've said, this whole idea may be really new to you, and your ego is likely to resist it. So that's what we will explore in Chapter 3. You've spent a lot of time and energy *not* feeling good and blocking your Super Attractor power by comparing yourself to others and investing in the illusion of lack. I'm taking on these blocks in the coming chapter. I'll give you my methods for kicking comparison, competition, jealousy, and overachieving. And I'll show you how to call in abundance with mind-set shifts that work fast.

Chapter 3

THERE'S MORE THAN ENOUGH TO GO AROUND

For many years I've led a training called the Spirit Junkie Masterclass. This training helps spiritual people gain the confidence and business-building tools to inspire others by doing what inspires them. It attracts people from all professions and backgrounds. I've met lawyers, yogis, life coaches, therapists, nurses, makeup artists, and more. They come from different places in the world and are at different points in their careers and lives. But they all start the training with one common desire: to make an impact in the world and be abundant doing it. I've trained thousands of people with my methods, and I've seen radical transformations.

My students begin their Spirit Junkie Masterclass journey revved up, inspired, and excited to step into their power. But I've noticed a number of common fears and forms of resistance at the beginning of the training. Many students don't feel like they're good enough or have enough resources to do the big work they want to do. Many people say they feel unqualified or lack the time, money, or support they deem necessary. Still others fear that their ideas have been taken. They say things like "She's already doing this, so how can I?" Many students arrive with the mantra "Who am I to do this?" Masterclass alumni reading this book are likely nodding their heads in recognition! Showing up for your dream takes guts, and it can bring up a lot of fear.

This fear mentality shows up in all of us, especially when we're on the precipice of something great. Fear of not having enough and fear of not being enough are both major blocks to our Super Attractor power. Many people suffer from feelings of lack that have been ingrained in them since childhood. Or they constantly compare themselves to others and see everything as a competition. I've fallen prey to these thoughts and behaviors, and I'm sure you have too. These types of fears are easy to succumb to.

Comparison is an especially difficult emotion to navigate. Most of us know that it's not helpful to compare ourselves to others. But what many of us don't know is that comparison is actually a form of judgment, and judgment weakens our attracting power. It doesn't matter whether we are judging someone because we view them in a negative way or because they have something we may want. It doesn't matter whether we're putting them on a pedestal and admiring what we deem to be their superiority. The fact that we're judging at all means we are unconsciously telling the Universe that we *don't* want what they have.

This might sound completely counterintuitive. But when you're envious of what someone else has, or when you see someone as somehow better than you because of what they have, you lower your energetic vibration. These feelings of comparison and judgment cause us to vibrate at a low frequency, repelling the very thing we want.

The fear, lack, and comparison I saw in my Spirit Junkie Masterclass students are things I took very seriously. I recognized these blocks as ones I had struggled with too, and I looked at the ways I had cleared them in my own life. I then adjusted the training to have a strong focus on confidence and alignment with the Universe. In order for my students to serve in the big, meaningful ways they desired, they needed to release the beliefs that held them back and kept their vibrations low. I started by helping them understand how their lack and comparison were blocking their Super Attractor power.

Here are the seven blocks I identified in my students. We all have these blocks, and they show up in sneaky ways. There may be some you identify with immediately and others that you may be ignoring. This is an opportunity to get honest with yourself. We can't harness our attracting power until we know how we block it. Taking a truthful inventory of the ways we block our Super Attractor power will bring conscious awareness to how we can return to it. Don't be afraid of these blocks, as they're common and most of us are unconscious of them. Our awareness is what heals the patterns that hold us back from being Super Attractors.

BLOCK #1: BELIEVING IN LACK

If you harbor feelings of not being enough or not having enough, you expend a lot of effort trying to prove to the world that you *are* enough. All that effort blocks the flow of the Universe. When we spend our energy trying to prove ourselves to the world, we lose track of feeling good—because we're trying so hard to feel *good enough*. The constant attempts to feel *good enough* come off as needy energy. This low-level energy repels the things you want. It repels the support of other people, it repels your own creative ideas, and it repels inspiration from the Universe. The time and energy you pour into trying to prove your worthiness become part of the reason why you don't receive what you want. All your effort to be seen keeps you living in the shadows, denying the light of who you truly are. The great news is that there is a way out of this lack mentality. A way out of the low-level energy. A way out of the shadows.

BLOCK #2: THINKING THERE'S NOT ENOUGH TO GO AROUND

The idea that there's not enough to go around is a pervasive fear. In this fear state, we struggle to get what we want and take pride in our overachiever behavior. We believe that we have to get as much as we can before someone else takes it. We imagine a zero-sum situation in which there's only so much to go around. This mentality, while it might spur us into action, can just as likely paralyze us. Many people avoid taking action on their desires because they fear the potential for disappointment. When you believe there's a limit to abundance and joy, you may avoid trying altogether. But when we shift from a world of lack to a world of abundance, we can remember that *there's more than enough* to go around. When you approach the world as a vibrational reality rather than a physical space, that's when your desires become real. When you're able to access the energy of abundance and have faith that the Universe always provides, you can begin to feel your desire come into form before it shows up in the physical world. We can't have one foot in the world of lack and one foot in the world of abundance. Our work is all about alignment. When you're aligned with the Universe, you know anything is possible, and lack fades away. Every practice in this book will help you tune in to the frequency that allows you to recognize all the abundance around you. When you're tuned in to the energy of abundance, you become abundant.

BLOCK #3: COMPARING OURSELVES TO OTHERS

A big block to our Super Attractor power is when we compare ourselves to others. At some point we are all guilty of this behavior, and it's understandable. All we have to do is open a social media app for a constant stream of opportunities to compare. Your inner voice of fear likes to use comparison to stop you from claiming what you desire. That fear-based voice wants to keep you "safe," playing small and minimizing perceived risk. But you lose your power to attract when you compare. Your Super Attractor power comes from how you feel, your faith in love, and your joy. When you're comparing, your focus isn't on how you feel, your faith in love, or the happiness you emanate. Instead, your focus is on what you have or don't have, all that you're lacking, and all that you think you need in order to achieve. If your focus is on the outside, then you'll constantly compare yourself to those who seem to have what you want.

Each time you compare your circumstances with another person's, you reinforce feelings of inadequacy. These feelings are so strong that they attract their likeness. Here's an example: imagine you are the last in your group of friends to be engaged. If you desire a committed relationship, comparing yourself to your engaged friends will leave you feeling terrible. That feeling will not support your attracting power. Rather, it strengthens the momentum behind your fear of being single. Energy goes where your intention flows, so when you're focused on all your friends having what you want, you end up manifesting more of what you don't want. Remember, your Super Attractor power comes from how you feel, your faith in love, and the joy you put out.

BLOCK #4: THE NEED TO WIN AT THE EXPENSE OF HAVING FUN

The Universe is an all-inclusive stream of abundance, and there's enough for everyone. When we become competitive, we cut off the stream of abundance. The fear of losing or the need to win is really another form of lack, one that implies scarcity. Many people pride themselves on their competitive nature, but it can create resistance. They make their happiness and sense of success dependent on "winning." Even when it comes to "healthy competition," a shift in perception can be very valuable. While some people may thrive in sports or business because of their competitive nature, I challenge you to consider a new idea. What if you shifted your focus off of the need to win and the fear of losing and onto how much fun the activity brings? This simple shift will put you into a state of joy, which inevitably brings far more success.

For the past six years, I've been part of an annual competition. The last two years found me at the top of the leaderboard with ease and grace. Last year, shortly after the results were in, I got on a call with the woman who came in second. She jokingly said, "Gabby, I love you, but I still can't get over that I'm in second place! I am very competitive." I said to her, "The reason for my success here is because I wasn't competing." While it's awesome to finish first or win a big prize, it wasn't my primary focus. I can honestly say that the reason I won was because my energy was surrendered, my focus was on having fun, and I didn't care about the outcome. I wasn't some strategic mastermind. I just enjoyed the process. I share this because I want to emphasize that it's safe to have big dreams and not care about the results! In fact, the moment we release the results, we let the support of the Universe back us up. We let go and allow.

But competing at the expense of having fun is the opposite of letting go. If you need to win in order to feel good, happy, or successful, then competition only creates separation, judgment, attack, inner turmoil, and a belief in lack. When your happiness depends on the score, you're sending a message to the Universe that you need to be "better" than someone else to feel good enough. That energy is never supported. I'm not saying to drop out of all competitive activities. Many people derive a lot of pleasure, joy, satisfaction, personal growth, and interpersonal bonding from competitive activities. What's important is your answer to this question: How does competing make you feel? If the fear of losing perpetually looms in the back of your mind, and you feel joy only when you win—and that joy fades as you gear up for the next competition—then competition is a block to your Super Attractor power. Wouldn't it be nice if you could achieve and succeed with grace and ease? When you redirect your competitive energy, you can have fun no matter the outcome.

BLOCK #5: FEARING REJECTION

I've witnessed many people deny their dreams due to fear of rejection. The idea of being rejected can be paralyzing. Many of us have come to see rejection as a form of humiliation or defeat. However, there is another way to view it. I've learned to see rejection as a form of protection. I trust that when something doesn't work out the way I planned, it's because there's something far greater in store for me.

Here is an example from my professional life. I had been presented with what seemed like a fantastic opportunity. I was really psyched as we contemplated an exciting plan. But the lawyers were taking a long time to negotiate every detail of the contract. New versions were constantly being drafted, but none of them seemed to incorporate our ideas or needs. Six months of negotiations went by, and in many ways I felt as if we were going backward! Frustrated by the situation, I decided to open up to seeing things differently. Instead of trying to make something that felt wrong work, I chose to see the situation as guidance from the Universe. When I took a step back, it became obvious to me that the issue was not the nitty-gritty elements of the deal; there was a fundamental lack of understanding as to what each side wanted. All the resistance we'd received along the way wasn't rejection. It was guidance. We were being led to not do the deal. Two years later we look back on this offer and celebrate how it fell apart! I am grateful for the lawyers getting in the way, and we know that the Universe was just guiding us in the right direction.

I encourage you to open up to the idea that rejection is protection. Choosing this perspective will help you dissolve your fear of rejection. If you choose to see rejection as guidance, then what is there to fear? If you get turned down by someone you asked on a date, it's because someone better is on the way. If your offer on a house falls through, it's because that house wasn't for you. If you make it to the final round of interviews for what you've decided is your dream job and someone else gets the position, guess what? It wasn't your dream job.

Accepting rejection as guidance gives you another opportunity to follow the flow of the Universe and strengthen your faith in a plan better than your own. Most importantly, you'll no longer fear rejection. Releasing that fear will give you the freedom to dream big, take fearless action, and let life lead you. Follow the guidance you receive, even when it feels like rejection. You'll be surprised. Rejection can be the greatest guidance of all.

BLOCK #6: HAVING A NEED-MORE MENTALITY

Do you ever feel as though once you achieve a goal, you immediately have to move on to the next one? Not feeling complete in the moment of achievement, do you keep reaching toward the next goal? The need-more mentality is another form of lack. It suggests that you may be looking for something outside yourself to feel complete rather than trusting in your completeness now. The outside search for success, accomplishment, and approval is an addictive pattern that keeps us out of alignment with the Universe.

We block the support of the Universe when our focus is on a future achievement. The ups and downs of needing more can be really depressing. You may get a high the moment you achieve something, but the buzz of the achievement is short-lived and quickly replaced by the fear of failing to reach your next goal.

I lived with a need-more mentality for decades. I'd achieve one goal only to be immediately obsessed with the next. My husband worried that I never took time to celebrate my success or be really present in the moment. I was achieving because I believed in myself, but I wasn't enjoying the journey. Let me pause here for a moment, because it's important to point this out. If you believe in your ability to achieve your desires, then they will come into form. Having faith in your ability is important, but it's *far* from the only important thing. If you're not having fun along the way, then what's the point? Ultimately, living with the need-more mentality blocks you from reaching your full potential. Marianne Williamson often shares this message, inspired by *A Course in Miracles*:

> The people who have achieved the most on earth have achieved a fraction of what all of us are capable of. Whatever you've done, either great or small, it is TINY compared to the potential that still lies within you.

We block our real achievements when we don't enjoy the journey. When I stopped living from achievement to achievement and started focusing on the fun along the way, my life got great! I started to feel more connected to my friends, my husband, and my work. I was more present, and life began to flow. I relaxed and let myself celebrate the miracle moments. When I dropped the need-more mentality, I achieved SO MUCH more than I thought possible! When we enjoy the moment and let the Universe flow through us, we are guided to create what God intended rather than what we think we need.

BLOCK #7: THE FEAR OF BEING JUDGED

Another big block to your Super Attractor power is the emphasis on what others think. I've seen this block reveal itself in many of my friends and students. My students have big dreams of sharing their spiritual work with the world. They see themselves writing books, speaking on stages, and spreading empowering lessons in their own unique ways. But a fear of being judged holds them back. They tell me that their family and friends don't believe in their career path or dreams. My response is, "The only reason they don't believe in it is because you still don't." I help them to see how their lack mentality and disbelief are being mirrored back to them by others. Our vibes attract our tribe. Embodying an energy of lack and self-judgment sends out a message to others that we don't feel good enough or worthy of what we desire. That energy can be felt miles away. The people in our lives (especially those who are closest to us) can be great spiritual teachers because they reflect back to us the energy we're putting out. Their judgment of us is a reflection of what we feel about ourselves, whether consciously or unconsciously. But when we return to faith and believe in our desires, then the world can believe in us too. And even if everyone doesn't fully co-sign your desires, your faith will be enough to tone down their judgment and shift their energy. Maybe they stop resisting your visions, or they curtail their judgment of you. When you release your resistance, you will feel released by others. Recognize that other people's judgments reveal the places where you lack faith. Every experience and encounter offers you guidance toward healing the lingering resistance that holds you back from being a Super Attractor. So rather than blaming others for resisting your dreams, thank them for showing you an opportunity for great growth and healing.

Lack, doubt, comparison, and insecurity stand in the way of attracting our desires. But there is a way through each of these blocks. Now that you have a greater understanding of each block, I'm going to break down the methods for change. This is the fun part, and I'm excited to share these methods with you. I've witnessed countless people experience radical shifts by following them. Try these methods, and you'll see for yourself how quickly you can move from an energy of lack to an energy of faith. There's no reason for you to play small anymore. The Universe has big plans for you, and it's time to claim them.

THE UNIVERSAL ABUNDANCE METHOD

Protect your desires to stay in alignment

It's important to avoid comparing your desires or emotions with others. Attracting what you desire is about alignment with the Universe and assuming the energy of how you want to feel. Put your feelings above all else, and respect your feelings by keeping them close while you're in the process of strengthening your faith.

One way you must protect your desires is by creating clear, loving boundaries with anyone who resists them. It's not uncommon to find that people in your life have a pre-conceived notion of who they think you should be or per-haps who you used to be. These projections from others can take you out of alignment with the Universe. When you find your desires challenged by others, respond by creating com-passionate boundaries. Those around you don't even need to know that you're creating these boundaries if you do it with love. For instance, if you're prompted to talk about a desire before it's ready to be shared, you can kindly say, "I'm cur-rently developing some new ideas and projects. They mean a lot to me, so I'm not going to share about them until they're fully developed." Or you can request that certain topics be left alone completely. For instance, when I was trying to conceive, I had to lovingly ask my mother not to interfere. I kindly told her that her actions were (inadvertently) triggering a feeling of disappointment. I asked her instead that we talk about other topics. Because I created this boundary with love, she was able to hear me and respect my desires. And I was able to protect my dream and stay connected to feeling good.

In some instances, it's impractical to create loving boundaries. In those situations, you can consciously dis-engage from people who bring you down energetically. For example, if you're healing a condition, don't go online and read through message boards filled with other people's stories about that illness. If you're trying to attract more money, limit your time with those friends who constantly talk about their financial problems. If you want to mani-fest a new partner, don't engage with people who are always complaining about their relationship dramas. If you're ready to step into a new passion project, don't share it with some-one who you know to be pessimistic. I've made it my priority to choose friends, team members, and partners who believe in my visions. I have no space in my life for anyone who stifles my flow. Protect your dreams no matter what.

Another way to protect your feelings and emotions is to keep your visions to yourself before they're fully developed. Let's say you're ready to make a career change, or you're open to dating again following a breakup. While you hopefully feel empowered and excited by these desires, they may still be backed with an energy of lack or bring up fearful past experiences. That voice of fear may be louder than the loving voice of your inner guidance system. That's why I suggest you nurture your desires by keeping them to yourself until you feel faithful and aligned. If you share your desires from a place of misalignment, they'll be met with resistance. Remember, the Universe is picking up the energy you put out. So when you share your desires with an energy of fear, people will respond to you with more fear. Sharing your desires from a place of fear or uncertainty will weaken your attracting power. Instead, keep your desires close while you're still strengthening your faith.

How will you know when you're ready to share your visions with the world? You will develop a strong sense of connection and certainty around your desire, and that's when you'll know it's time to share. And when you present your ideas with conviction and belief, the people around you will support your ideas (even those who didn't or wouldn't in the past). The Universe will always reflect back to you the energy you vibrate outward. Abraham-Hicks say:

> This is a universe of diversity, and diversity means plenty to go around, and source energy will answer everyone. And it's only in your shortage consciousness where you believe that there is a finite amount of resources that you're squabbling over. The resources that you're reaching for are infinite, and your ability to achieve a desire for something means that the Universe has the ability to deliver it to you with no exceptions.

There are no exceptions. Maintain alignment with love, and you will receive.

Focus on giving rather than getting

I have an amazing student named Stephanie. Stephanie went through my master class and was ready to hit the ground running. For her first event, she wanted to host a workshop at her local library based on a training I'd developed. Stephanie diligently created a syllabus and course lessons. In order to get the word out, she made flyers, sent emails, and talked up the workshop on Facebook.

The day of the workshop, she showed up to the library ready to rock, and instead of the big group of people she'd imagined, there was just one woman in the room. Stephanie felt let down and embarrassed, but with one person there, she couldn't just leave.

Walking up to her, Stephanie said, "Hi. Are you here for my workshop?"

The woman said, "No . . . what workshop?"

Fighting back tears, Stephanie said, "It's a six-part workshop based on a book called *May Cause Miracles* by my teacher Gabby Bernstein. I've been preparing an awesome workshop, and nobody showed up—but I'd really like to share it with someone."

The woman said, "I could actually use a miracle! Let's do it."

At that moment, Stephanie was forced to let go of the need to teach to a big group that day and instead focus on her true desire, which is to serve, by teaching the one woman in the room. And here is the important point: the moment Stephanie made it about service rather than about her ego, everything fell into place. She shifted from a "get" mentality to a "give" mentality and delivered an amazing workshop. It was a miracle moment in her life.

Stephanie could have taken an understandable but less healthy approach to this situation. But she found the courage to focus on the *content* rather than the *frame* of her experience. In that moment, she cared only about sharing the gift of her teaching. Later that day, Stephanie called to share her story with me. She was so excited to tell me about living her purpose and being in the light and joy of service that the size of the audience was an afterthought in her retelling. That day Stephanie shifted her energy in a major way by embracing the feeling of confidence and pride. This energy has continued to propel her forward as a successful coach, an inspirational voice online, and a powerful example for you today!

If you're stuck on the "frame" of how you think things should look, take Stephanie's story to heart. Redirect your focus from what you can get to how you can give. The moment you make this shift, a miracle will occur for you too. The Universe greatly supports your service energy and is always opening doors to that end. Focusing on the service will keep you from judging and comparing. You'll feel proud of your commitment! The fastest way to get out of an energy of lack is to give.

Each day ask yourself, "How can I serve?" Asking this question puts you into alignment with the Universe. I remember Dr. Wayne Dyer saying, "When you ask yourself, 'How can I serve?' the Universe responds, 'How can I serve you?'" Trust that when you offer up an energy of service, the Universe will send it back to you tenfold. You'll feel powerful in the presence of your service, and that power is what attracts.

Want more for others

Wanting more for others puts us into an energy of abundance. Why? Because it feels good to want others to feel good. The practice of wishing for others to receive expands your own ability to receive, and this feeling of abundance will help you to attract more of what you want into your life. When you genuinely want others to be abundant, the Universe will respond in kind.

Early in my career, I coached young women my age. Many of them were desperate to find their true loves and get engaged. They'd compare themselves to all their friends on Facebook posting pictures of engagement rings. I could relate—I was guilty of the same thing.

I knew I couldn't give them spiritual principles that I wasn't applying in my own life. I had to find a solution of my own before I could confidently offer it to them. So I decided to turn the story around. Each time I saw a friend post about her engagement, I'd let myself be happy for her. After all, no amount of jealousy was going to get me closer to my fiancé. So instead, I let the vision of my friend's joy inspire me to feel excited for my own engagement. I started celebrating the relationships around me. When I saw couples holding hands on the street, I'd let their love inspire me. I consciously chose to perceive loving relationships as a part of my manifesting journey. Instead of choosing to see their love as a reminder of what I *didn't* have, I chose to see it as a reminder of what I was creating. When you see others who have what you want, celebrate it! Let their success mirror back to you what you're ready to receive.

Wanting more for others requires that we release the block of comparison. When we compare ourselves to others, we lean into the lack mentality and the feeling that there's not enough love in the Universe to support us all. Years after I cleared this block regarding relationships, I hit a similar block trying to conceive. If you're someone on the path to conception, protect your attracting power by not comparing your fertility journey to others' or judging your friends who seem to have no trouble getting pregnant. I know this can sound impossible when you are in the depths of the struggle. But I promise it will lift you out of it.

I tried to conceive for three years. And for the first two years, as I struggled with my emotions, I'd get annoyed when my friends would talk to me about their babies, their nursing experiences, and all that went into motherhood. I felt like an outsider, which directed my focus back to my perceived lack. My constant comparison made me feel depressed. Deep down I knew that a baby couldn't be conceived out of the energy of neediness and that I had to change my ways. So I decided to shift my focus off of what I didn't have and onto celebrating what my friends did have. Instead of comparing and judging, I let other women's mothering energy fill my heart. I asked them questions and spent time with their children. I stopped comparing myself to my friends who had children, and instead I started celebrating their motherhood. I'd spend time asking about their pregnancies, holding their babies, and learning their parenting tips and strategies. I celebrated motherhood alongside my friends, and their reality started to feel like my reality. Even though my baby had yet to arrive, I let myself be in the positive expectation of what was coming. The more I assumed the positive energy of motherhood, the closer my baby felt.

The source of our envy is a part of us that we haven't yet developed. If someone has what you want, this doesn't imply that it's not available to you. In fact, it's the opposite. Your envy is a reflection of your deep desire. Even if your ego has convinced you that there's not enough to go around, your Higher Self knows the truth. Transform your jealousy into clarity. Turn it into an opportunity to clarify to the Universe what you really want. I believe that the more you see others who have what you want, the closer you are to getting it. Choose to see the people who have what you want as a reflection of what's to come. See them as gentle winks from the Universe revealing the future to you. Pay attention to the people who are thriving in areas you want to thrive in. Accept that their miracles are yours. The more you allow yourself to feel good about their greatness, the faster it comes into form for you.

Do something, anything, that brings you joy

Yes, this again! Remember, the key to manifesting is to feel good. I'll repeat this countless times throughout this book. The quickest way out of lack is to lean toward what feels good instead. Focus on your primary desire, which is to align with the joy of who you are. If you find yourself stuck in a story of lack or comparison, keep it simple. Just choose to focus on something that brings you joy. When I get caught up in a story of lack, I cook, go for a walk, exercise—anything that takes my focus off what's not working and redirects it back onto what feels good. Your belief in lack and comparison can be very strong. It feels like it's impossible to change. But the reality is that the moment you do something, anything, to feel better, you're instantly catapulted out of the lack. The goal isn't to miraculously shift your perception (though we'll welcome this type of miracle). The goal is to think and feel your way out of lack one thought at a time.

Turn on the faucet

Start to keep track of each time you successfully shift from fear back to love. As you add up the miracle moments, you build momentum behind your practice. Direct your thoughts toward what's working and thriving and away from fear, lack, and resistance. In any moment, you can practice the Choose Again Method and reach for a better-feeling emotion. Directing your focus onto what's thriving creates more of what you want and strengthens your faith in the Universe.

Applying the practices within the Universal Abundance Method will elevate your attracting power. You'll transcend the energy of limitation and embody the energy of prosperity. Healing your lack mentality realigns you with joy and helps you accept the abundance of the Universe. Deciding to feel good, let go, and release attachments aligns you with the flow of the Universe. Saying yes to the Universe is like turning on a faucet—all that you need will come to you. Focus on the process rather than the outcome. All the outcomes we desire show up when we're in the flow. Shifting from comparison to oneness, from competition to compassion, and from lack to love will bring you into flow fast.

Let the Universe support you. Feel confident knowing that what others have is a reflection of what is on the way for you. Celebrate other people's successes generously and sincerely!

THE PROMISE OF HEALING LACK

Healing your lack mentality promises many benefits. When your thoughts and energy are no longer stuck in lack, the Universe can provide. Life is no longer a race from one achievement to the next. Instead, life becomes about the moment-to-moment experience of feeling good. Dr. Wayne Dyer famously said, "You do not attract what you want; you attract what you are." Don't become the lack that you so greatly want to avoid. Instead, assume the feelings of joy, abundance, and prosperity to become a Super Attractor.

The methods in this chapter will bring you a lot of relief. Think about all the time you've spent feeling jealous, anxiously comparing, fearing lack, and future tripping. That is all behind you! Going forward, you can celebrate other people's success, accept the greatness that comes to you, and enjoy the present moment knowing that what you want is on the way. When you kick the habit of lack and separation, you will feel free.

It's empowering and exciting to know that your thoughts and feelings have the power to attract your desires! This feeling will be emphasized in Chapter 4. I'll teach you a method that will help you swiftly move from low-level thoughts and energy to a more positive state. I'll guide you to trust in the power of your thoughts and energy to help you navigate the tough moments in life. Follow my guidance, and you'll be amazed by the results.

Chapter 4

HAVE FUN
ALONG THE WAY

One Saturday morning in June, I went to a friend's house for breakfast. It was a sunny, beautiful weekend day, and we made a delicious meal together. But while I was relaxed and enjoying myself, it was clear that she was nervous and distracted. As we sat at the table drinking coffee, I asked her what was wrong. She told me that later that morning she was taking her 9-year-old son, Jack, to a baseball tryout. He'd find out that day whether he'd be moving up to the "majors" or staying in the "minors." She was worried that he wasn't going to make it and that he'd be devastated. Out of the corner of my eye, I caught a glimpse of Jack. He was standing in the living room, overhearing our conversation. I saw the fear in his eyes, and I could sense his discomfort. My friend looked over at him and said, "Jack, the only thing you need to do today is have fun. Don't worry about what happens. Just have a good time!"

I could tell he wanted to believe that. But his nervous expression told me that that his fear of not getting picked was stronger than his desire to have fun.

Jack headed off to tryouts, and when he returned a few hours later, it was obvious from his body language that he had not been picked. The sad energy was palpable. Instead of trying to let it blow over, I went over to Jack. I said, "I understand you're disappointed. Tell me how you feel." I let him rant. He went on about how unfair it all was. How the boy who got moved up was smaller, younger, and not as good. Jack built up a tremendous amount of energetic momentum around the negative story. At first the spiritual teacher in me wanted to do anything I could to relieve him of his pain and bring him back to a good mood. But Jack was really digging in. I wasn't going to get this 9-year-old boy from despair to carefree happiness all that quickly.

In situations like these, we almost never leap from misery right to joy. But we *can* lift ourselves out of a low-vibration energy bit by bit. I like to refer to Abraham-Hicks's Emotional Guidance Scale (shown below). The idea behind the emotional scale is that while you can't usually go from a low vibration to a high vibration right away, you can make small moves up the scale. Attainable, better-feeling thoughts and energy help you climb the scale to a joyful place.

Your emotions are a direct indicator of how much you're resisting or allowing. When you're in an energy of joy, you're allowing yourself to be a Super Attractor. The closer you are to the emotion of joy, the more easily you attract what you want. But what do you do when you're really far from a feeling of joy? In these situations it's not wise to try to leap up the scale as fast as possible. If you've ever tried to force yourself to do it, then you know how hard it is. In fact, trying to go from a very low vibration to a very high vibration quickly might leave you feeling worse. When you're in a negative place, high-vibe thoughts won't resonate—they'll just feel false. So instead of trying to leap, we have to lovingly guide ourselves back to joy. Returning to joy is a gentle process that requires small steps up the emotional scale.

The emotional scale is a list of commonly felt emotions ranging from joy, appreciation, freedom, love, and empowerment (the highest) to fear, despair, desperation, grief, and powerlessness (the lowest). The goal is to identify where you are on the emotional scale and proactively reach for better-feeling thoughts that lead to better-feeling emotions. Once you stabilize in a new emotion, you've moved up the scale! Then you continue the practice of reaching for a better-feeling thought and moving up the scale to a higher-vibration emotion.

The emotions you feel become the energy you emit. Your energy is important because it's your point of attraction. So when you're low on the emotional scale, you're emitting negative energy and attracting people, situations, and experiences into your life that match that vibration. This is why we say things like "My day went from bad to worse" and "I'm in a negative spiral." We're always attracting and manifesting, even if it's unconscious.

As you lift yourself out of a low-vibration state and move up the emotional scale, your point of attraction shifts with every step. When you lean toward joy in any situation, you literally change the vibrational frequency of what's happening around you.

Listed below is the emotional scale as described by Abraham-Hicks.

THE EMOTIONAL GUIDANCE SCALE

1. Joy/Appreciation/Empowered/Freedom/Love
2. Passion
3. Enthusiasm/Eagerness/Happiness
4. Positive Expectation/Belief
5. Optimism
6. Hopefulness
7. Contentment
8. Boredom
9. Pessimism
10. Frustration/Irritation/Impatience
11. Overwhelment (feeling overwhelmed)
12. Disappointment
13. Doubt
14. Worry
15. Blame
16. Discouragement
17. Anger
18. Revenge
19. Hatred/Rage
20. Jealousy
21. Insecurity/Guilt/Unworthiness
22. Fear/Grief/Desperation/Despair/Powerlessness

Here's how I used the emotional scale with our little baseball player, Jack. When he walked in the door, he was clearly in fear, grief, desperation, despair, and powerlessness. I knew he might stay stuck there all day and possibly longer if he didn't have some guidance to get out. So I sat down with him, compassionately honored his emotions, and let him rant. I then gently guided him to reach for thoughts that lifted him up the scale just a bit. I said, "How does all of this make you feel?" He said, "I feel bad because now I'm the oldest person on my minor league team."

In that moment Jack's discomfort with being the oldest on the team moved him up the scale to insecurity/guilt/unworthiness. I said, "I understand how you feel. I imagine you're mad." He replied, "Yes, I'm really mad because it's not fair! The kid who got picked is younger and smaller than me. The coaches didn't follow the rules!"

Jack had moved into jealousy, then zoomed right up to hatred and rage, and even into blame. I could see a small amount of relief come over him as he went from despair to rage. It's funny to think that rage could be an improvement, but it has a more positive energy than fear/grief/desperation/despair/powerlessness. When we understand this, we can see how moving from despair to rage is progress!

What he said about the coaches not following the rules told me he was moving up the scale to blame, so I coaxed that out of him a bit. I asked, "What else are you upset about?" He stabilized on blame as he complained about the coaches who didn't pick him. Then on his own, without any guidance from me, he moved into worry. He said, "I'm worried I won't get a lot of time on the field because they'll want to give the younger kids a chance to play." He shrugged and sighed.

At this point, Jack was resolved to sit with his disappointment and didn't want to continue talking about the situation. But he was clearly feeling slightly better now that he'd moved out of despair.

Later that day, we all went to the soccer field to watch Jack's younger brother play. I was chatting with Jack's mom at the field when I noticed Jack roaming around aimlessly. He came up to us and said, "I'm bored."

I was so excited to hear this! I knew that boredom was a huge leap up the emotional scale. Leaving the field, Jack rode back with my husband, Zach, and me. During the drive, Zach got him talking about cars—a subject Jack is passionate about. They went on and on discussing everything from dream cars to various racetracks. I could hear excitement and enthusiasm in Jack's voice. Thoughts of the baseball tryout were far from reach. He had now moved up to the energy of passion without even realizing it. Abraham-Hicks say, "Distraction is the fastest way back into alignment." We naturally move up the emotional scale when we're distracted by something that makes us feel better than the negativity we previously focused on. If we're really stuck in and upset about something, it can seem hard to let anything else get our attention. But a simple distraction can be a miracle. The moment you (even slightly) shift your focus onto something else, you'll feel better.

In the 12-Step community, it's often suggested that the best way to get out of your own drama is to be of service to someone else. I've applied this practice for years. Whenever I notice myself obsessing about an issue that's upsetting, I shift my focus quickly by checking in on my friends to see how they're doing. I'll pick up the phone, call a friend, and say, "How are you? How can I support you right now?" The moment I get into the energy of service and focus on someone else is a miracle. The miracle is that I've shifted my perception and distracted myself from my own dramas. Best of all, I've helped someone else!

Distraction really worked for Jack. By the time we got home, he was dancing around the house, playing on the computer, and telling jokes. He was back in joy! Even though an earlier disappointment had him really down, he was able to emotionally guide himself back up the scale and return to joy. This little man was a miracle worker.

Let Jack's story inspire you! The next time you notice yourself at the bottom of the emotional scale, gently practice reaching for better-feeling thoughts and emotions. Know that you can move up the scale bit by bit, step by step. And as this example demonstrates, you can and often will move up the scale by focusing on something other than what's upsetting you. This doesn't mean you're ignoring difficult emotions or checking out of tough situations. In fact, it's quite the opposite. By moving up the emotional scale, you can more easily attract the support, solutions, ideas, and perspective shifts you need to resolve problems and move through your feelings in a productive way.

Let's look at another example. Maybe you've been killing some time on Instagram but quickly find yourself feeling envious and dissatisfied over your perceived lack. Pretty pictures of vacation photos and designer clothes have you feeling simultaneously jealous and ashamed of your jealousy.

Finally, you put down your phone because you're just too angry to keep looking. Don't be afraid of this anger! In fact, celebrate the shift. Anger is a higher-vibration emotion than jealousy. Going from jealousy to anger is a clear sign that you're moving up the emotional scale. Now your work is to keep climbing.

Sometimes you can just let your emotions ride out, and you'll naturally find your way back up the scale. Other times you may need to be more proactive in choosing a new thought and energy. If you find that you're going down the scale or you're stuck in a lower-level vibration, the solution is simple. Return to the Choose Again Method from Chapter 1 and add the Emotional Scale method from this chapter.

Let's do a quick recap of the Choose Again Method:

1. Notice the thought.

Notice when your thoughts and energy are out of alignment with joy, and ask yourself, "How do I feel right now?" Review the emotional scale and take note of where you're at.

2. Forgive the thought.

Forgive yourself for being misaligned, and celebrate your desire to shift. Thank your negative feelings and thoughts for showing you what you don't want and revealing what you do want.

3. Choose again and guide yourself up the emotional scale.

Answer this question: "What is the best-feeling thought I can find right now?" If you're really low on the scale and can't think of anything, ask the Universe to guide you toward that better-feeling thought. Remember, the thought can be totally unrelated to the reason for the emotional state you're in. When that thought makes you feel better, reach for another one. Gently guide yourself back up the emotional scale. Thinking about anything better than where you were will get you to where you want to be. Remember how positive it is to move to another emotion, even if that emotion doesn't seem joyful yet. Don't overthink this process. Abraham-Hicks simplify it by saying, "All you have to do is figure out what you want and talk yourself into it." Keep it simple, and reach for the next best thought that leads toward what you want.

The process of reaching for a better-feeling thought may be very foreign to you. Maybe you're like me, and you've spent years in therapy digging up old fears and memories from the past. Or maybe you're someone who's tried to work out issues by feeling into your uncomfortable emotions.

While I greatly believe in traditional therapeutic healing, I also know that if I begin that healing from a higher vibrational stance, I won't get caught in the stories. Once I heard Eckhart Tolle say in an interview that if you're focusing on a negative past experience, you can choose to recognize that the experience is no longer happening now. The moment you choose to focus on the safety and security of the present moment, the past can dissolve. With this process you're honoring your negative feelings, but you aren't dwelling in them. This is an important distinction! Most of us either ignore or skim past our feelings or wallow in them. With this process you honor your negative feelings but choose to move to a better feeling fast.

For many of us, moving up the emotional scale requires a fundamental perspective shift. I'm still exploring its effects, even years into this process. It's okay if you're having a little trouble wrapping your mind around the emotional scale and the process of climbing it. Be willing to try it anyway. You're likely to feel great relief.

Part of what makes the process so powerful is that you don't have to force yourself back to joy in order to reclaim your positive momentum. You just have to be honest about how you're feeling and choose the next best thought. Your willingness to feel better will be your guide out of despair and into joy. Feeling your feelings is essential to moving up the scale. Often when we're stuck in an emotion, the reason we can't get out of it is that we're unwilling to acknowledge what's really going on. The second you honor your true feelings, you experience relief and can move into a new vibrational stance.

Practice this regularly. Whenever you notice you're stuck in low thoughts and energy, return to the emotional scale, choose again, and guide yourself back. Each time you choose again and reach for the best-feeling thought you can find in the moment, you're gently moving up the scale and into alignment with the joyful vibrations of the Universe.

FIND JOY IN ANY SITUATION

Our resistance to joy blocks us from attracting whatever it is we desire. When we embody an energy of joy, we release resistance. I recognize that it can be difficult to find joy in seemingly joyless situations, but it's far more painful to live a joyless existence. So many of us inadvertently live that way, whether by focusing on what's not working or by frequently complaining about our circumstances. We hope complaining will make us feel better or at least help us find a sympathetic ear. But when we focus on what's not working, we just get more of what's not working.

One of the fastest ways to guide yourself back up the emotional scale is to do something that makes you feel good. If I've had a bad day, I'll pick out some music, grab my headphones, and go for a walk around the block or hit the gym. I've learned through experience that even if things aren't going the way I planned, I can still have fun. In fact, the more fun I have, the closer I get to attracting what I want. Sometimes we have to stop focusing so hard on our desires in order to attract them into our life. It's not that we ever lose the desire. The desire is always with us. It's just that focusing on its absence actually deflects it, whereas having fun brings us closer to receiving our desire. Taking the focus off your desire and redirecting your energy toward joy shifts you to a more positive point of attraction. Think about the last time you were obsessing about something you wanted. It probably didn't feel joyful. All your focus and attention toward what you don't have creates resistance. Release the grip of that resistance by redirecting your focus onto something fun that will distract you. Fun can come from the simplest acts. Exercise, call a friend you love, do a crossword puzzle, or spend quality time playing with your child. If an activity brings you a sense of satisfaction, contentment, warmth, excitement, or happiness, then it's fun. As soon as you lean into a fun and joyful experience, you move yourself up the emotional scale.

An easy way to create more fun throughout the day is to smile at people and engage in random conversations. I'll talk to literally anyone. I'll walk down the street and tell a mother how beautiful her child is. Or I'll strike up a conversation with a stranger about his or her day. These spontaneous moments of connection can bring forth a lot of joy for everyone. Maybe you're not like me, striking up conversations with random people, but you can smile at someone on your commute or offer to get your co-worker a coffee. These seemingly insignificant moments of connection catapult us back into our true love nature. Embodying joy and love is what being a Super Attractor is all about. I want to emphasize that it's not hard to reclaim your Super Attractor connection. One moment of happiness is enough.

Instead of seeking out these opportunities to feel good, we often stifle our full expression of joy by focusing strongly on an outcome. Fixating on a specific outcome that we think we want causes us to struggle and suffer as we attempt to force it. We don't let ourselves feel happy, satisfied, or relaxed until we can check that goal off the list. Even if we do achieve the goal, we immediately zero in on the next task to accomplish. Living from achievement to achievement is an addictive pattern that holds us back from truly enjoying the richness of life. When we make fun a priority and release outcomes, we can stop complaining and start attracting. But I see so many people get hung up on the idea that joy comes from achievement. This is backwards! The goal isn't to achieve something but to have fun along the way to what you desire. Assuming an energy of joy is the fastest way to achieve success! For instance, if you're trying to attract a romantic partner, be sure to have fun on those dating apps or on that blind date. This is especially true even when you feel that any particular date isn't for you. There are still so many opportunities to learn something new and interesting about the other person or yourself. If you bring joy to the process, you'll maintain a positive point of attraction, which will speed up your capacity to manifest the partner you desire. Your fun energy is sexy, and it will be felt on every date (and even through those apps)! There's nothing more attractive than someone who's having fun.

If you want to manifest a new job, find ways to have more fun in the job you currently have. The good energy you bring to whatever work you do helps open doors for new opportunities. This might seem counterintuitive, especially if you don't like your current job. You might be thinking, "How can I possibly enjoy this place? I hate my job!" But finding a better one will require your attracting energy, and so you will have to shift your perspective on your current job. Can you be friendlier to co-workers? Can you bring more ideas and enthusiasm into meetings? Can you make your desk/office a more high-vibe space? When you start to make these shifts, you'll find that you'll feel better about your current situation, and everyone you encounter will feel better about you. From this place of positive energy, you will attract that new job much faster!

If you're out of alignment with the physical well-being you desire, make your healing process fun. I've found great success healing myself when I chose to have fun cooking medicinal foods and practicing self-care. A beautiful example of this is my best friend Jenny, who's been helping her father, Ray, through his chemotherapy treatment. Every step of the way, Ray has maintained a positive attitude. He shows up for his treatment with enthusiasm and optimism. He cracks jokes with the nurses and keeps the mood light. And he spends time with Jenny researching healing foods that will nourish him. I know that Ray's attitude is not only making the experience easier but also sending a message to every cell in his body by releasing any resistance to his healing. His joy clears blocks, supports his physical body and his mental state, and keeps him open to creative possibilities for healing.

Make it your priority to have fun even when things aren't working out the way you planned or when your manifestations haven't arrived yet. Trust that the more fun you have, the more you speed up the manifesting process. Having fun along the way shifts your energy to certainty. When joy becomes your default, you become certain that everything will work out, even if the end result is different from what you planned. You'll learn to rely on your own capacity to access joy rather than needing it from an outside source. No romance, amount of money, credential, or achievement can give you the sense of certainty your own joy can provide. When you practice having fun along the way, the Universe supports you. The support, flow, and synchronicity you receive from the Universe give you a great sense of certainty. Choosing fun will help you remember that you're being guided by an ever-present force of love. It will give you freedom to rely on the Universe and trust that joy will clear the path.

You may be thinking, "How can I find joy when I'm really down about something?" Always remember that you don't have to leap toward joy. You gently guide yourself up the emotional scale one step at a time. Abraham-Hicks say, "Don't let any place that you are standing frighten you." Let it inform you. The energy you're in right now offers you clarity about what you truly want.

JOY OPENS INVISIBLE DOORS

One of my favorite hobbies is cooking. I'm a self-taught, "intuitive" chef. I don't use recipes, and I've created my own techniques. I feel free in the kitchen, and cooking has become another form of meditation for me. I've spent years documenting my meals on social media through photos and blog posts, so when Instagram Stories came out, I was off to the races. Most evenings I share video tutorials of whatever I'm cooking for dinner—I call it the Gabby Cooking Show. Each recipe I share brings me happiness. I include the mantras that I listen to while I cook, and the fun I'm having comes through the phone screens of thousands of viewers throughout the world.

I started the Gabby Cooking Show out of sheer enjoyment and nothing else. It was an authentic expression of my favorite hobby. Within a few months of regularly sharing, interesting things started to happen. I began receiving outreach emails from food brands that wanted to send me kitchen appliances for the Gabby Cooking Show. People started coming up to me at my events and telling me how much they loved my meal ideas. And then one night at a friend's party, something really funny occurred. Across the room I saw a young woman walking toward me. She seemed happy to see me. I thought she must have been a reader excited to share her experience of one of my books. But to my surprise she said, "Oh my God! You're that girl with the Gabby Cooking Show! I love it." I laughed out loud. I found it amazing that, of all the things I've done in my career, I was being recognized for a little Instagram show that I set up on a whim!

Today, take some time to do something that brings you joy. Find your own Gabby Cooking Show. Do something that lights you up, and witness how the Universe supports it. I can hear some of you complaining that you just don't have the time. First, you have to make feeling good a priority—you owe it to yourself and those around you. Second, you only need a few minutes for things like journaling, meditating, going for a walk, listening to your favorite song, or striking up a conversation with a co-worker or neighbor. Give yourself at least two minutes of reprieve every day from the incessant fear-based belief systems that keep you in negativity. A few minutes is all it takes. Remember, the moment you lean toward joy, you're led up the emotional scale.

Introducing joy to a situation changes the vibrational frequency of what's happening around you. Try this out. The next time you're annoyed in that long meeting or sucked into a gossipy conversation at brunch, crack a joke. Bring joy into the joyless environment, and watch the energy change in the room. You are a shapeshifter. Think about the mornings you enter the office in a good mood—I'm sure people treat you with more kindness and higher vibes than on the days when you show up with a bad attitude. You have the power to shift the energy around you by choosing to be in joy. Even when other people don't start off in that place, you have the power to lift them up with you. Anytime you bring your high-vibe energy to someone in a lower vibration, they will be elevated in your presence. Often what matters most isn't even what you say or do but the energy you give off. Be the person who lights up a room!

CARRY A FLASHLIGHT

Many of my students ask me how they can maintain their high vibes when the people around them are stuck in negativity. My response is, "Always carry a flashlight." It serves as a constant reminder of your ability to shine light even around the darkness of others.

Shining your light is the best way to deal with negativity. We sometimes think that commiserating is the most effective way to help. But commiserating only makes things worse. If someone is suffering, you don't want to bring your energy down to help them feel better. Does it make you feel good to be pitied? Probably not. Being pitied usually perpetuates our discomfort and reinforces our sense of powerlessness. We think, "Things must *really* be bad if they think so too." Instead of pitying someone, turn on your inner flashlight, maintain your high vibration, and guide that person back to peace through your positive presence. Your high vibration will brighten their world. When you get aligned with the energy of joy, you become a bearer of light for everyone you meet, and you give others inspiration to shine when they're around you. Aim to be a source of light in the world simply by assuming an energy of joy. In the presence of your joy, others will recognize their own.

CALIBRATE YOUR ENERGY TO A POSITIVE FREQUENCY

All the greatness I've attracted into my life has come from high-vibrational energy. In 2015 I declared that I was going to measure my success based on how much fun I was having. In several of my books, I've written about the power of fun and the magnetic force field of joy, and I've long said that happiness is a choice I make. But I've recently made it an even higher priority. This is when I began to really feel the fluidity of joy in my life. I accepted that joy can be a feeling I tune in to all the time, not just in fleeting moments. This big shift occurred when I became devoted to my well-being and committed to the power of positive thinking, stress reduction, and releasing resistance. Living these practices wholeheartedly allowed me to recalibrate my energy. I'm no longer striving for moments of joyful relief; now I feel the flow of joy throughout my days.

The shift for me was that I decided to stop giving purpose to my pain. I honored my suffering from the past but chose to no longer dwell in it. I decided to be new and accept joy as my birthright. This newness showed up in my work, my marriage, and my physical health. As soon as I decided to live with ease and joy, my life changed forever. In a short period of time, I felt like a new person. This is the happiest I've ever been. I share this with you because I know this miracle awaits you too. When you are guided to a book like this, it's because you have a strong desire to feel better. That desire is enough for you to experience a miraculous shift. You can decide today to recalibrate your energy and commit to love and joy. In an instant you can choose a world beyond your fear. I know this to be true because many of you have reached out and shared your experience of it with me. When you embark on a spiritual path, a shift occurs whether you're conscious of it or not. And if you stick to the path and stay committed to your practices, one day you wake up and you're new.

Welcome your newness now. If you've taken the time to apply even one of the principles in this book, you're new. These methods recalibrate your energy and bring you back up the emotional scale. The simplest shift is enough to set you on a new path. Pay attention to your newness, and celebrate each shift, no matter how small. Celebrate the moments when you choose to relax rather than push harder. When you forgive rather than attack. When you choose a better-feeling thought and think your way out of despair. These seemingly minor moments are the miracles. Be proud of each miraculous shift. Thank you for your commitment.

RIDE THE WAVE OF POSITIVITY

Even the slightest shift in your energy is enough to redirect your energetic flow toward joy. When you feel that shift, let it take over. Take it even further, and feel it as much as possible. The moment I notice my energy inch closer to love and joy, I reach for more. I feel the good vibrations and let them move me deeply. I consciously continue reaching for more and more positive thoughts. It happens frequently when I'm driving in the countryside, listening to mantra music. I often get a hit of great wonder as I pass forests and fields, listening to the sounds of the music. When I feel this feeling, I ride the momentum and keep the good vibes flowing. I start to think about how grateful I am to live in a peaceful community and how much I love that I can drive to the local farm and pick up food for the week, feeling free behind the wheel. I think about the dinner I'm going to cook later that night and how much my husband will appreciate it. I go even further and start sending love to my friends in my community and celebrating the great connections I've made. I then honor myself for committing to serving the world. I let this joy move through me. Riding this momentum is a really fun process.

The next time you feel your energy begin to calibrate toward love, ride the wave of positivity, and then take it even further. Let your thoughts flow with more and more joy. Reach further and further for more good-feeling emotions. You can't take this practice too far. Surf the wave of positivity, and don't stop. Feeling good is the goal, so when you get there, go grab even more of it!

INSPIRE OTHERS BY DOING WHAT INSPIRES YOU

You may still be feeling some resistance to the idea that having fun is one of the most important things you can do. This is a normal reaction. Many new spiritual students fear that their spiritual path is selfish. They feel guilty taking time for fun and being unapologetic about their desires. But one of the greatest lessons I've learned from Abraham-Hicks is that we must be selfish in our practice. "Selfish" here is not a negative concept. This kind of selfishness doesn't hurt anyone else, and it doesn't mean you neglect others in any way. But it requires you to put your joy first. You must make your joy your highest priority. When you're selfish about your well-being, you're actually being of high service to the world. This is because the more joy you embody and the more you allow inspiration to move though you, the more powerfully you will serve others. We can't help or uplift anyone or anything else from a place of resistance and low vibration. The greatest gift we can give is our positive energy. So I'm encouraging you to become more selfish about how you want to feel. Trust that the happier and more inspired you are, the more you can give to your family, your friends, your co-workers, and your community.

We're living in a time when we must bring more positivity and light to the world. Anyone on a spiritual path has signed up to be of service. The first service is the energy you bring. Great change in the world cannot come from our hopelessness; it must come from our inspiration and joy. When we make our joy a priority, brilliant ideas will come naturally, support will surround us, and movements will form. People who are truly happy are also truly helpful.

When you know how amazing it is to live in joy, you can't help but want to spread it. As you embody this energy, you will lift the veil from a world of fear to reveal a world filled with light. This is the practice in the next chapter. In the coming pages, you will learn that there is a world beyond the fearful perceptions we've grown to rely on. There is a world of peace, happiness, freedom, and light. Get excited to lift the veil.

Chapter 5

LIFT THE VEIL

When I was a child, I was very aware of a world beyond my physical sight. I believed in angels and fairies, and I was highly intuitive. When we're very young, there is no veil between the physical world and the spiritual realm. This is why you'll often hear kids speak of angels or talk to their imaginary friends. They may even talk about past lives or intuitively predict something that they couldn't have possibly known. In this state of innocence, little ones can perceive a world beyond the limitations of the body and see with spiritual sight.

As a young child, I trusted in myself and a higher power. Over time that faith was taken from me as the fears of the world grew louder. I started to feel alone, insecure, and afraid in a world full of fear and limitation. There were many moments that separated me from the love of the Universe. Witnessing my parents go through a divorce, being bullied on the playground, and sometimes getting low grades in school were among the experiences of separation that built up my worldview of fear.

As we grow into adulthood, the spiritual realm becomes harder to access. We weave a veil between the Universal realm of spirit and the physical world we've grown to rely on. We begin to identify with our bodies rather than our spirits. We are taught, and often encouraged, to make this change by our parents, teachers, and others around us. As we get older, almost everyone and everything we encounter seems to reinforce a world of separateness and fear. Each fear-based thought we're exposed to strengthens our belief in the physical world and distances us from the spiritual realm.

Thankfully, no matter how far I detoured into the fear of the world, I always knew there was more beyond the physical. That knowledge saved me from feeling adrift and alone. Even in my darkest hour, I believed that with a spiritual connection, anything is possible. As a spiritual student, I've made it my daily devotion to lift the veil of the physical world and remember the light of the spiritual realm. This daily devotion has given me great peace amid the tension and turmoil we all encounter. The practice of choosing to see with spiritual sight has become a habit. I use it to remember that the Universe is guiding me, and I restore my thoughts back to love. Without this spiritual connection, I'd get lost in the world of fearful projections.

One of the ways I've stayed committed to seeing with spiritual sight has been through writing. Over the past decade, I've written seven books on spiritual principles. In these works, I go out of my way to translate and demystify spirituality so that it will be easy for anyone to grasp. While I believe this has been greatly helpful, as I write this book, I feel called to push the metaphysical envelope. Every word I write here reminds me of what I know to be true. Channeling the words in these books brings me so much joy because the process lifts the veil between the worldly and spiritual realms. In order for all of us to truly accept that we are Super Attractors, we must embrace a world beyond plain logic and reason. We must become willing to be unapologetic about what our faith in the Universe means to us.

I want to guide you to lift the veil between the world of perception and the world of spiritual connection. Beyond the veil of the fear-based world, there are miracles waiting for you. You haven't blocked them—you just haven't been looking for them. Lesson 91 of *A Course in Miracles* says, "Miracles are seen in light."

The *Course* teaches:

> The miracle is always there. Its presence is not caused by your vision; its absence is not the result of your failure to see. It is only your awareness of miracles that is affected. You will see them in the light; you will not see them in the dark.

It's time for you to see with light.

As long as we remain convinced that the physical world is our only reality, miracles will remain unseen. We've been encouraged to focus on this physical world of form, which has put us into a habit of denying the light. As a result we've blinded ourselves. All we perceive is the darkness we've created. From childhood we've created a worldview based on fear, separation, judgment, and scarcity. It's as though we're living in a nightmare—but all we have to do is turn on the light in order to recognize it's just a bad dream.

Our belief in our perception of ourselves, our physical bodies, and all the fears of the world makes it hard to believe in love. We believe we're unsafe, susceptible to disease, attack, and pain. Our faith in the body has kept us living in fear. We believe in stories of illness, trauma, deprivation, and hate. We believe the story of separateness, thinking we are better than some people and inferior to others. These belief systems occur when we disconnect from the love of the Universe. One separate thought leads to the next, and they multiply in our minds. *A Course in Miracles* suggests that we thought up a "tiny mad idea" of being separate from the Universe, and this began a lifelong separation from love. The tiny mad idea is that we are separate from the love of the Universe, or as the *Course* would say, God. When we took the tiny mad idea seriously and believed it happened, we decided that the love of the Universe was not enough. We chose to believe that we could create a love based on a separate world of duality. When we chose the tiny mad idea, we turned our backs on the love of the Universe. At this point the ego convinced us that we were unsafe and therefore responsible for making up a world and thought system that would make us feel good enough. To make matters worse, we feel guilty because we have separated from our truth, which is love. We chose to believe in the identity of the separate self, which makes us believe in a world that is disconnected from love. The moment we took the tiny mad idea of separation seriously, we chose a world of fear over love.

The way out of that fear is to lift the veil and see through the lens of spirit. When we do this, we will remember that we are safe, whole, and protected. When we accept that there is a world of love and support beyond our physical realm, we can see ourselves as spirits having a human experience. This spiritual perception can bring us great peace, love, and joy. This is the concept of heaven on Earth—when we live in the world but think with the thoughts of heaven.

When we perceive a world of separation, we unconsciously feel a sense of guilt for turning our backs on what the *Course* calls perfect love. Each tiny mad idea of separateness builds up a dream world disconnected from the truthful love of who we are. We become overwhelmed with self-hatred for the separated self that we've become, because on an unconscious level, our belief in separation makes us guilty, defensive, and alone. These beliefs are what make up the veil hiding us from our Super Attractor truth and the love of who we are.

As the *Course* explains, the tiny mad ideas of separation aren't the problem. Rather, the problem is the way we respond to them. When we respond to fear-based thoughts with more fear, we perpetuate the separation from love. Each day, we choose to lean into tiny mad ideas of separateness with beliefs such as "I don't have enough," "Everyone is out to get me," "I'm better than them," "I am unlovable," and so on. From the moment we wake up, we're crafting a dream world of separation and distancing ourselves from our truth.

The question then becomes: Why don't we all just lift the veil? If on the other side of the veil are light, love, and truth, what are we waiting for? Why has it taken us so long?

The answer is that we're terrified of turning on the light. Because who would we be if we weren't a body stuck in the dramas of the world we've created? We've grown to rely on the perceptions we've built up against love, and we use them to protect ourselves from disappointment and pain. If we merely lifted the veil to love and released our worldly perceptions, that pain would dissolve.

Even with my faith in the spiritual realm, I am constantly challenged by my perception of my self-image, my body, and the separation from love. One month before I began writing this book, I hit a major low point in life. I'd been sick for months with an undiagnosed stomach condition. I was in a lot of pain, I couldn't eat anything, and I was obsessed with finding solutions. I spent countless hours Googling my symptoms and diagnosing myself, which is a terrible idea that I do not recommend. I was praying and meditating, but my fear was louder than my faith, and I continued to be obsessed with my body. Finally, after months of testing, I got an answer about my condition. At first this clarity brought me some relief. But almost immediately I began fixating on how I'd heal myself. I knew in my heart that my bodily obsession was perpetuating the problem. So I began to pray for relief.

My prayers were answered over lunch with my friend and teacher Marianne Williamson. Marianne asked me how I was doing, and I launched into a monologue about all the pain and suffering I'd been going through. I told her that I finally had a diagnosis, but I complained that there was a long road to recovery. My energy was frantic, and she could sense my fear. She looked me in the eyes and said, "You're obsessed with body identification." Marianne reminded me that I could identify with the part of me that was going through this struggle (the body), or I could identify with the part of me that *wasn't* going through it (the spirit). She reminded me that the body heals when we're not looking at it.

Marianne's words guided me back to truth, and to a lesson from the *Course* that says, "I am not a body. I am free." This was a tough concept to embrace when my physical symptoms were activated. But I knew that as long as I was identifying with my body, my symptoms couldn't subside. I looked more closely at how this physical condition came about. A series of loveless moments of separation had caused me to feel a lot of stress. That stress directed my focus onto the world, my body, and my false, fear-based perception of myself. I forgot my true purpose, which is to be love and extend love.

I took Marianne's advice and chose to identify with spirit. Living with spirit identification didn't mean I stopped taking medication or following a healing protocol. But it meant that I stopped insistently focusing on the body, which was keeping me in the dark. I prayed to see myself in the light. I meditated on the vision of lifting the veil and standing in the ever-present light of the Universe. Shifting from body identification to spirit identification gave me faith in my ability to attract good health. I followed daily, devoted practices to help me lift the veil and cross the bridge from my perception of the world to a world of light. Each day I continue to remind myself that "miracles are seen in light." Each prayer brings me closer to the light, each meditation redirects my energetic frequency toward the light, and each loving thought clears the path back to the light. I have accepted that the love within me reveals my light. I don't have to clear away the darkness; I just have to choose to see in light.

I know you understand the difference between body identification and spirit identification on a soulful level. But on a worldly level, you'll resist it. The *Course* says, "To be told that what you do not see is there sounds like insanity. . . . Your faith lies in the darkness, not the light." I deeply understand this existential struggle between the world of darkness and the spiritual realm of light. I still live with so much emphasis on a world that I don't want to see: a world of attack, hatred, anger, and resentment. A world of struggle, pain, disappointment, and suffering. But I've come to believe that the only way out of that world of darkness is to choose to see the light as often as possible. Seeing the light is a practice, and it requires our willingness to suspend our disbelief. We must get into the habit of seeing with light.

The more we tune in to the vision of light, the more the perception of darkness begins to fade away. *A Course in Miracles* even speaks of "light episodes." Several years ago I was sitting on a beach reading the *Course*. I set the book down in my lap and looked out at the ocean. As I gazed at the place where the water meets the sand, I began to see a bright, rectangular frame of light in the sky. It was as if I were looking at the ocean through this white-light frame. I was initially startled but also comforted by the sight. As it dissipated, I looked back down at my book and saw this passage in the *Course*:

> You will begin to understand it when you have seen little edges of light around the same familiar objects which you see now. That is the beginning of real vision. . . .
> As we go along, you may have many "light episodes."

I smiled with a sense of knowing that there was indeed a world beyond my physical sight. Since that time I've had many light episodes. I see bright sparks of light, and I see streaks of light dance through the air like tinsel. Often I see light in my meditations. When I slow down and realign with the Universe, the light is revealed as a deep inner feeling. I love these light episodes because they remind me that I am not a body; I am free.

These days I look for the light wherever I go. I can't block it, but I often detour into fear and forget to look for light. The light is always there, and it's my choice to see it. I wish for you to have your own experience of the light episodes. I want you to know the true meaning of living in this world but thinking with the thoughts of love. I want you to be able to bridge the world of perception and the world of light. And I want you to bring that light back into this world of perception so you can help to expand our limited vision— to brighten the darkness. When we live in the light, we remember that we have Super Attractor power. We know we can connect to a presence of strength, wisdom, and peace beyond the world.

Now, don't freak out. I told you this was going to push the metaphysical envelope. Right now, tap into the part of yourself that believes in the light, or even in a desire to believe. This will guide you to begin this journey of undoing the perception of darkness and remembering the light. If you're resisting anything about this chapter, just tune in to the part of yourself that believes in love and stay open to a new perspective.

We tend to make our spiritual practice very complicated when it's not at all. What's complicated is our resistance to it. Suspend your disbelief, if only for the duration of this chapter, and let me help you remember the light. It's time to lift the veil. Follow my guidance and keep it simple.

DON'T JUDGE YOURSELF FOR PERCEIVING DARKNESS

Let's begin by releasing any self-criticism or attack. I've seen so many people judge themselves for how far they've detoured into fear and darkness. Remember, the light never left you. The world of darkness you perceive is merely a series of tiny mad ideas and loveless moments that have disconnected you from the light of who you are. Right now, accept that the darkness and discomfort have been great opportunities to get closer to spirit. Let yourself off the hook for the ways you've bought into the fear of the world. Forgive yourself for all the ways you've chosen to believe in darkness. Forgive your attack thoughts, forgive your self-judgment, forgive your wrongdoings, and forgive yourself for fearing the light. Remember what the *Course* teaches: "Miracles are seen in light." The moment you choose to shift your thoughts from fear to love, you will experience a miracle. Choose it now by forgiving your fearful thoughts so that you can return to spirit.

CHOOSE TO SEE IN THE LIGHT

Whenever you get hooked into the perceptions of the physical world, ask yourself, "Do I wish to see this in the dark, or do I wish to see this in the light?" If you have the willingness to ask this question, then you'll have the

willingness to choose the light. The moment you ask yourself this question, you invite a spiritual presence beyond
your own to guide your thoughts back to love. The question is a prayer for help. It's a reminder that there's a world
beyond your physical sight, a world beyond fear, a world
beyond limitation, a world that is bright. The vision of light
is waiting for you to choose it. Consciously choose to see
with light all throughout the day. Make this a habit.

Many miracles arise when you make this simple choice.
I recently experienced a miraculous shift by choosing to see
with light. One afternoon I received an email from someone concerned about a hateful post about me on someone's
Facebook page. A woman had written a long rant about how
I was a fraud. You can imagine how devastating this was for
me to read. What upset me most was that several people on
her page chimed in with comments. People said things like
"Finally, someone is speaking up about how awful Gabby
is." Typically I don't react to hate on the internet. I have
prided myself on a practice I call "forgive and delete." But
this post really triggered me. I spent hours stuck in the
darkness of this negativity. I scrolled through other negative
posts on this woman's page, I got defensive, and I let myself
feel depressed about it. Later that night, while I was still feeling really down about the post, my husband called me out.
Zach said, "Are you still obsessing about that?"

I said, "Yeah. I can't seem to shake it."

He looked at me with great compassion and said, "Stop
reading her negative feed, and go help the people who want
to hear from you. Start with the thousands of direct messages sitting in your Instagram inbox."

This was the miracle. I felt so much relief the moment
he suggested that I redirect my focus off the darkness and
choose to see the light instead. So I made my husband show
me where to find the direct messages in Instagram (I had

no idea!). I didn't know the light was there because I wasn't looking for it! I then spent the next few days responding to the most beautiful stories, testimonials, and messages from people all throughout the world. People had been sending me notes of gratitude, prayers, and miraculous stories. During those few days responding to posts, helping people recommit to their spiritual path, I felt full of light and purpose. I felt deeply connected to my community and infused with joy. I had disconnected from my perception of my body (physical self), which could be attacked, and I had reconnected to my spirit, which is a force of love in the world.

I woke up on the third morning filled with love. Instead of picking up my phone or jumping out of bed, I immediately thought, "Pray for the people you've been connecting to." I went into deep prayer. I started to send light to my community. I prayed for them to have peace of mind, health, joy, and their own spiritual awakening. I prayed for them to remember the light. I'd never felt more joyful in my life. The hateful comments on Facebook had faded away and held no power. I truly understood that "miracles are seen in light."

This experience transformed me. Redirecting my focus off the negativity and on to how I could serve others was the catalyst for a great spiritual awakening. I could see clearly in the light and forgive the projections of others. Today I can say that I am deeply grateful for the women who were hating me on Facebook. They offered me a divine spiritual assignment and a miracle. I know that they can feel my love because I have released them. I love them for showing me that light can cast out all fear.

In this experience, I was able to identify my own core value. I came to realize that what I value most about myself is my ability to be a presence of love in the world. When faced with darkness, I was able to access the light by helping other people feel good. I came to see how, when we're in a place of resentment or reactivity, we're merely defending against the light. The only response to fear is love.

I hope my story helps you see how simple it is to lift the veil on the darkness of negative thoughts and reclaim your light. In any moment you can make this choice. When you feel bullied, choose to focus on how you can make others feel good. When you feel weak, focus on your strength to follow your spiritual path. When you're outraged by the injustices of the world, focus on the practices in this book to realign yourself with your light so you can shift from an energy of separateness and return to love. Where there is darkness, may you bring light.

BE PROUD OF YOUR CHOICE TO SEE LIGHT

When you stop focusing on the physical self, you can see through the lens of spirit. You'll begin to care less about the issues that arise and care more about how you choose to handle them. Each time you ask yourself, "Do I wish to see this in the dark, or do I wish to see this in the light?" you open the door for a miracle. Begin to measure your spiritual maturity not on how easy your life is but on how easy you are on yourself when things go awry. Celebrate the miracle moments when you shift from body identification to spirit identification. Ride the momentum of the miracles, and let the joy of living in the light envelop you. When you have any experience of trading fear for love, you will build up spiritual proof that spiritual sight is what you really want.

MEDITATE IN THE LIGHT

It can be tough to choose the light when we're hooked into worldly drama. That's where meditation comes in. There's a popular misconception that meditation is just for relieving stress or silencing your racing thoughts. It does do that—but it does so much more too. When we meditate, we can transcend the energy of this world and step into a place of love. Meditation becomes a pathway to the light. You surrender your will to the loving presence within and can be gently guided over the bridge from the world of perception to the world of light. Meditation will offer you a reprieve from attachment to fear. This may sound mysterious, but you'll know it when it happens. The more resistance you release on your meditation pillow, the more you'll know the world beyond your physical experience. You can let healing occur, allow creative ideas to surface, and invite a feeling of gratitude to shower over you. I want you to know the immense relief and joy that comes when you meditate in the light.

The pathway to alignment with the Universe begins with the stillness found in meditation. This is a stillness so deep that you leave the world of perception behind and step into the power of your light. In still meditation you can suspend your fearful perception of the world, even if it's just for a moment. A moment is enough. A moment of faith can change you forever. Through meditation you'll establish your own experience of the light beyond the fears of the world. You'll experience the miracle that has been waiting for you. Your connection to this nonphysical dimension will enter into every corner of your life. It will help you effortlessly maintain a positive flow of well-being and abundance to attract more of what you want.

MEDITATION FOR LIFTING THE VEIL

Follow my meditation for lifting the veil. As soon as you come out of this meditation, open your journal and write about your experience of the light. It's important to document this experience so you don't forget.

Meditation for lifting the veil

(To listen to the free audio version of this meditation, visit the resources page GabbyBernstein.com/SuperAttractor for a free instant download.)

Find a comfortable place to sit on the floor or upright in a chair.

Gently close your eyes, and place your hands on your lap, facing upward.

Breathe in for a count of five.

Five Four Three Two One

Breath out for a count of five.

Five Four Three Two One

Breathe in for a count of five.

Five Four Three Two One

Breath out for a count of five.

Five Four Three Two One

Continue this cycle of breath, and allow yourself to fall gently into a peaceful state.

Let your thoughts come and go. Do not judge them.

Continue to breathe in for five and out for five.

As you breathe, see yourself standing at the edge of a bridge, about to step onto it. The bridge can be low to the ground or high off the ground.

Behind you is a shadowy cloud of darkness. You can sense that this darkness represents your fear and your bodily perception of the world.

As you look ahead over the bridge, you see a bright, glimmering light. This light has an energetic pull drawing you toward it.

Take a deep breath in and release as you surrender to the powerful energetic pull of the light.

Let the light draw you toward it as you begin to walk across the bridge from the darkness into the light.

Breathe in and out with each step.

As you get closer and closer to the end of the bridge, you begin to notice the shadows of the world disappear.

You can no longer see them behind you.

Take a deep breath and step off the bridge and into the world of light.

Now all you see is light.

In this light you are not your body, you are free.

You are an energy field of love and light.

You are powerful.

You are peaceful.

You are supported.

You are loved.

You have no past resistance and no fear of the future.

All you have is the light in this moment.

Give yourself permission to stand in this light for as long as you want.

Continue to breathe long and deep, and let the light restore you back to the truth of who you are.

Stand in the light and breathe.

When you feel called to come out of your meditation, say a silent prayer to yourself: "Miracles are seen in light. I choose to see in light and bring light with me wherever I go."

Take a deep breath in and release.

When you're ready, open your eyes.

Following your meditation, pick up your journal and write freely about your experience of standing in the light. Document the miracle of releasing the world of fear and accepting the world of light. You'll find great value in this practice because it will be a way of reminding yourself of who you truly are.

When you've finished your free-writing exercise, say your prayer one more time: "Miracles are seen in light. I choose to see in light and bring light with me wherever I go."

Now go about your day, and bring light with you wherever you go.

This meditation is enough to help you see with light. You may have an experience of a light episode, or you may feel a sense of love and light come over you in meditation. It doesn't matter whether you see light with your physical eye or you feel it as a presence of healing. You will experience light in your own unique way. There are many beautiful ways to experience the light. Trust the way it comes through for you, and turn to it as often as possible.

The way we lift the veil of darkness and remember the light is to rely on the power of the Universe to restore our thoughts back to love. When we exchange our disbelief for faith, we remember the light. When we meditate, quiet our minds, and release resistance, we remember the light. When we choose compassion over attack, we remember the light. When we pray for forgiveness, we remember the light. When we choose to lift the veil of fear, all that's left is light.

BRING THE LIGHT WITH YOU WHEREVER YOU GO

When you begin to see past the fear-based world, you'll want to lean toward the light as often as possible. This will get easier and easier. You'll also feel called to bring that light with you wherever you go. You'll find purpose and contentment in being a beacon of light in your home, workplace, and community. You may even find that people are more drawn to you for support and guidance. It feels good to be around someone who's shining bright.

In this new role, you may feel the desire to help those who are suffering. If so, and when you notice someone struggling, it will be necessary for you to resist the need to get hooked into their drama. Parts of you may still identify with their need. But if you meet their need with more need, you cannot be of service to them. The best way to support someone stuck in fear is to lean into love and be the light.

You must meet them from a place of love and trust that your good-feeling energy is enough.

It's our souls' purpose to help others and bring light wherever we go. But we must consciously serve from a place of strength and alignment. Abraham-Hicks say, "You must be in alignment with their success as you offer assistance, and not in alignment with their problem." The best way to serve others is to feel excited and eager to guide them toward solutions rather than staying stuck in their problems. Your attention to their success aligns you with the fact that they, too, are Super Attractors. Your seeing them in this light helps them remember who they really are. Even if they're not ready to receive your guidance, your positive thoughts and energy are sufficient. Seeing someone in their wholeness is the greatest gift you can give them. Sometimes the best way to help someone out of the fear is not to do anything, but instead to visualize them surrounded by light.

THE LIGHT IS WHERE YOUR TRUE POWER LIES

True power lies in your spiritual connection and your capacity to tune in to the energy of love and the inner vision of light. True power is not some worldly credential, status, or achievement. Being a Super Attractor means we must lay down the things we think give us power in this world. All of our "outer power" is actually a defense against the light. When you think with the thoughts of love and see through the lens of light, you will find a way through every block. You'll no longer be a match for negativity, attack, judgment, or pain. Living with true spiritual power means living in the light.

I hope these messages have inspired you to begin to lift the veil of the fear-based world of suffering and embrace a world of faith and love. As we close this chapter, I want to remind you not to expect yourself to live in the light all the time. Even a fleeting moment of light is enough. As you add up the moments, they become your reality. Remember that this is a practice of undoing our dark perceptions and remembering our light and true power. It doesn't happen overnight, so it's important to celebrate the miracles along the way. Each shift in perception from dark to light brings you closer to truth. Let these shifts come naturally, and stay committed to the light.

In the next chapter, I'll help you get into further alignment with the light through the power of spiritual guidance. When you lean toward the light, you'll become aware of the Universal energy that is always supporting you. The presence of spiritual guidance was available to you as a child, and it's time to reconnect to it. You'll be guided to lift the veil and return to the loving support of a guidance you once believed in. Open your heart and mind to be receptive, and become willing to be supported.

Chapter 6

INVISIBLE GUIDANCE IS AVAILABLE TO YOU

One afternoon a good friend called me. From the moment I heard her voice I knew she was devastated. She told me she'd broken up with her boyfriend after trying hard to make the relationship work. In the end, there were fundamental issues that they just couldn't navigate. As much as the breakup hurt, what really scared her was that she didn't know what direction her life was headed in. She kept saying, "How did I get back here again?" She was vulnerable, defeated, and hopeless. I could feel her anguish and heartbreak over the phone. It was clear that she was totally out of alignment with her faith in the Universe. I tried to talk her out of fear and panic by helping her see that solutions were available. I relied on my practical mind, giving her advice on where she could live, what she might do about her finances, and how she could make some positive change. But all of it was only making her more depressed and overwhelmed.

After talking for well over an hour, I was emotionally exhausted and frustrated with her resistance. I was trying to help my friend, but so far I just wasn't getting through. I knew there had to be a better way, and I wanted to find it.

Without giving it much conscious thought, I found myself saying, "Have you asked your spirit guides for help?"

After a pause, she said, "No, I didn't even think of it . . . but to tell you the truth, Gabby, I never consider turning to spirit guides for help."

I told her about my own experience with spirit guides, how I never make a decision or go through any life transition without seeking their counsel. I shared with her that I believe there are many spiritual guides who are always working on our behalf. We all have our very own angel guide, who is there to protect us and guide us. We also have family members, teachers, and friends who have passed on and can help us. There are archangels whose sole purpose is to carry our thoughts and energy back into alignment with God. And there are countless other spirit guides and angels who are there for us whenever we ask. I went on and on about how I connect with my guides and how quickly I receive their support.

After several minutes of my spirit guides rhapsody, my friend said, "Wow, this sounds so *empowering*. I really love the idea of being able to ask for help." I could sense that her energy had shifted. There was relief in place of despair. She was ready to surrender her will over to the care of her guides and welcome spiritual support. By the time we wrapped up our conversation, she sounded like a different person. I know her guides were working through me to remind her of their presence. The moment she said yes to their support, she began to feel better.

The next day she called me again. "You'll never believe it," she said. "I took your advice and asked my guides for help. I had no idea who I was speaking to, but I prayed for help anyway. Then the most miraculous thing happened. Overnight everything started working out for me. I received an email about a freelance position, and I took the next step in planning a trip I have been putting off. I even feel a lot more peace around my breakup. My guides got to work fast!"

"Yes! That's what your guides want," I told her. "Their sole purpose is to align your thoughts and energy with the love of the Universe. When you're in alignment like that, you're a Super Attractor. That's how everything can fall into place."

Spirit guides and angels have always been a very important part of my life, but this is the first time I'm writing about them in a book. I've spoken of Universal guidance and God, but I've never fully given voice to the presence of my nonphysical guides. I was always worried I might freak people out or make someone feel like they had to share my beliefs. But as I said in the previous chapter, I feel called to push the metaphysical envelope and speak openly and unapologetically about the spiritual realm. I know the world is ready to open up to new forms of guidance. When we become willing to see a world beyond our physical sight, then life becomes easier, we feel safer, and we can access our true power. I accept that you may resist the concepts and lessons in this chapter. You may not believe in spiritual guides, or maybe you have your own beliefs that are contrary to mine. Or maybe this concept is totally new for you. I welcome your resistance, but I ask that you stay open. My goal for this book, and for everything I create, is to help crack you open to a spiritual relationship of your own understanding. I never aim to force my ideas onto you, but it's my job to always offer to you what I know to be true for myself.

So here goes. I believe there are beings of the highest truth and compassion working on our behalf to guide our thoughts and energy back to love. They are not physical and are not bound by the natural laws of this world. They are spiritual beings. These guides come in many forms, and they have different purposes. But their common goal is to help guide us back into alignment with the love of the Universe. When you get stuck in a fear-based thought or pattern, you can turn to your guides to help lead you back to love. To receive their guidance, all that's required is your willingness to surrender your fear and see with spiritual sight.

I've grown to rely on these nonphysical guides in every area of my life. Knowing that there is a presence always supporting me has given me unshakable faith and strength. There have been countless moments in my life when I've witnessed the divine intervention of my guides. A moment I've previously shared occurred on October 2, 2005, the day I chose to get sober. I hit bottom that day with my drug addiction. I was a 25-year-old woman strung out on drugs, crying on the floor of my studio apartment. At rock bottom, I found the willingness to pray for help. I said, "God, Universe, whoever is out there, I need a miracle."

Instantly I heard a powerful inner voice say, "Get clean, and you will live a life beyond your wildest dreams." The voice was so clear and undeniable that I had to listen. I got sober that day and continued to follow the spiritual guidance I received. I believed that these guides worked through other sober people and my recovery groups to help me stay clean. My slight willingness to surrender my addiction was all that was required for me to be led on a path of lifelong recovery. Day by day, moment by moment, I followed that guidance, and it led me to true healing. Today I truly do live a life beyond my wildest dreams. I know that inner voice I heard was the voice of my spirit guide. My guides were patiently waiting for me to find the willingness to open the door to their presence. Our guides are always prepared to support us, but we have to ask for help. Without our willingness we can easily miss all the guidance that is around us.

There are many ways to receive messages from spirit guides. When we open our consciousness to receive spiritual support, the most miraculous guidance will be presented to us. You may hear an audible voice or experience an inner knowing. You may feel the presence of a calming energy take over the room. In some cases you may feel physically pulled to do something. You might get guidance in a dream, or you might wake up in the middle of the night to receive a message. Guides have the power to work through technology, and they love using social media to give you direction and signs that you need. Your guides meet you where you are! They have many unique ways of bringing your thoughts back to love (God). For example, recently I was struggling to forgive someone who I felt had wronged me. I was obsessed with fearful perceptions of judgment and separation. I'd forgotten to see through the lens of love. My loveless thoughts kept me in a dark cycle of negativity. Finally, I became fed up with my lack of forgiveness and turned to my guides for help. Through a prayer I simply said, "Thank you, guides of the highest truth and compassion, for leading my thoughts about this person back to love." That was it. I just turned it over to my guides to show me what to do. Within 24 hours I began to receive guidance. I was scrolling through Facebook when a post from this person came up in my feed. Typically I'd scroll quickly past it or judge what she had written. But today was different. I felt an inner call to read her post. What she shared that day was exactly what I needed to hear to fully forgive her. She was sharing very vulnerably about her own personal struggles and all that she'd been through. She was showing a humanness I'd never seen before. In that moment I was able to see her through the lens of love and compassion rather than the lens of fear and defense. I was able to see her with spiritual sight. I know it was my guides who led me to that post that day. And when I felt the intuition to read her post, I know I was being energetically supported. In this instance they gave me clear direction to see her with love—and I allowed their guidance to come through by being willing to receive their direction. Once you become willing to turn over your fear to your guides, they will begin to lift the veil of fear and darkness, restoring your spiritual connection and leading you back to light and love.

Remember, our guides all share one main purpose: to lead us over the bridge from the world of fear back to the spiritual realm of love. And there are many ways they can help us get there. In this chapter I share several ways that we can feel the presence of guidance. Some of these forms of guidance may be familiar to you, whereas others may be new concepts. Pay attention to the types of guidance that light you up. Maybe you've never heard of archangels, but when you read about them, you feel a strong connection. Trust this. Whatever lights you up is speaking to you, and new guidance has begun.

THE LOVE OF THE UNIVERSE

Our inner wisdom and our spiritual guides lead our thoughts back to what I often refer to as the love of the Universe. This is the energy we tune in to when we're aligned with thoughts and feelings of love. When we're aligned with the Universe, we're connected to our Super Attractor power. Some people refer to this energy of love as Source or God. I think of the love of the Universe as a powerful, omnipresent energy. When you practice any of the prayers or meditations in this book, you're aligning your energy with the love of the Universe, and this force works in creative ways to guide you toward the highest good.

Sometimes when we feel stuck, blocked, or really down, we have a hard time feeling our connection to the Universe and we can't jump back fully into our faith. These are the times when we need spiritual guidance. So we call on spiritual support through prayer to lead us toward lessons and soulful assignments that will help us return to faith. *A Course in Miracles* says, "Prayer is the medium for miracles." When we pray, we surrender our will over for spiritual support. We open an invisible door, inviting spirit to step in and guide us back to love. There is no single way to realign with the love of the Universe, so remain open to discovering the unique ways you'll receive guidance. Remember, the goal is to surrender our agenda and open up to a spiritual relationship of our own understanding so that we can return to love.

YOUR HIGHER SELF

When we pray, we lift the veil of our fearful perceptions and welcome love. The guidance we receive through prayer presents itself in a number of ways, including a sense of knowing or an inner voice of intuition. At first, this inner voice may sound like a whisper, but the more you call on it, the easier it will be to hear. Ultimately, you will come to recognize this internal cheerleader as the voice of your Higher Self. Your Higher Self is always ready to speak up, but it must be given space to be heard. When you're bogged down by fear, controlling energy, and uncertainty, you're blocking your Higher Self.

Here is a prayer that will help you align with the profound wisdom of your Higher Self: *I surrender my fear and allow the voice of my Higher Self to guide me toward the highest good.* Use this prayer or feel free make up your own.

When you meditate, pray, and align with the energy of love, you're tuning in to your Higher Self. When you call on an angel, spirit, God, or the love of the Universe, you're asking to be guided back to your Higher Self. You're asking to remember the true essence of who you are. Spiritual guides are always ready to lead you back to this intuitive, inner knowing and faith in love. As I introduce you to several different types of guides remember that their job is to lead you back to your Higher Self. If the concept of spirit guides doesn't resonate with you, then know that you can return to your Higher Self anytime you choose to shift your perception through prayer, meditation, or any spiritual practice. The loving wisdom of your Higher Self is always there. You just have to tune in.

ANGELS AND ARCHANGELS

Angels are extensions of love on a mission to guide you back to your Higher Self and deepen your connection to the Universe. They protect you, guide you, and offer you great inner wisdom and healing messages. Angels are nondenominational and will help you in whatever spiritual or religious form resonates with you.

Many spiritual texts reference seven key archangels. The most well-known is Archangel Michael. Michael is the great protector and the most powerful of the archangels. It's valuable to call on Michael when you need protection of any kind. For instance, if you're afraid or concerned for your safety, Michael will be there to help you. You can call on Michael in a moment of crisis and he will offer immediate help in a form that will resonate with you. Michael offers great courage and guidance when you feel misdirected. And he loves to assist healers in performing their work. Often I experience the presence of Michael when I see a glimmer of cobalt blue light. At times I can even feel his presence, as though the room is expanding and a huge energy has entered into the space. Michael makes himself known if you're open to experiencing him.

Archangel Raphael is the angel known to aid in physical healing. He works to help you when you're sick, and if you're a healer or healthcare practitioner, he is always by your side, supporting your important work. Raphael will help you heal through new ideas and fresh information or even guide you to the right medical professionals to set you on your healing path. When it comes to mental health or addiction, Raphael will guide you to heal your root cause condition and help restore you to peace. He leads you toward inner harmony and physical well-being.

Archangel Gabriel is known as the angel for communication, serving as a messenger for God. I often call on Gabriel when I write and speak. He helps artists, writers, and teachers to carry their messages in authentic and meaningful ways. Gabriel will come to your aid when you're procrastinating or having trouble communicating. He's also a powerful guide in relation to children. He is the angel to call on if you're having trouble with conception, pregnancy, or birth. When I was trying to conceive, I continued to get messages from Gabriel that I was on the right path. One of those signs was a lily. Archangel Gabriel is often depicted holding lilies. During my conception journey, I would ask Gabriel to show me a lily to remind me that I was on the right path. One afternoon I opened my mail, and a reader had sent me a beautiful handwritten note. At the end of the note, he wrote, "I included in the envelope a prayer card. I kept getting a strong intuition that this was for you." I opened the envelope, and the prayer card inside was an image of Archangel Gabriel holding lilies. This sign was one of many lilies along my conception journey. If you're struggling with communication or motivation, or if you need support with a child, then call on Gabriel for help. You may even receive an unexpected bouquet of lilies!

If you're an animal lover or environmental activist, you'll want to connect to Archangel Ariel. She is known as the angel of nature, protecting Earth's natural resources, ecosystem, and all animals. Call on Ariel when you want to connect more deeply to nature. Invite her to join you on a hike, a walk in the park, or a swim. Her presence will give you a deeper connection to the planet and help you when it comes to healing the environment.

Then there's Archangel Jophiel, the archangel who supports artists and creatives. Jophiel will guide you to keep your thoughts pure and help you solve problems. Jophiel helps bring calm into our lives and clears away the chaos. As you use the practices in this book, call on Jophiel to help you manifest the beauty you desire in your life and in your mind. She will always be there to help you shift your perception and guide your thoughts back to love. When you need a new perspective or help with a creative endeavor, call on Jophiel for help.

Archangel Azrael is known to assist people when they're dying and helps newly crossed-over souls adjust to the spiritual realm. He also plays a very important role in helping people heal their grief when they've lost a loved one. If you're a spiritual teacher or religious guide who helps people healing from grief, be sure to call on Azrael to work with you and to protect your energy so that you don't absorb their sadness. But Azrael doesn't just help with the final transition. If you're going through *any* kind of change in life, you can call on Azrael for guidance.

Finally there is Archangel Chamuel, whose mission is to help bring peace to the world. I recommend you call on Chamuel when you're suffering from anxiety or struggling in a relationship. Chamuel helps us deal with adversity and gives us courage when we feel defeated and alone. Chamuel's presence is especially important today as we face so many challenges around division, adversity, and separation within communities.

Now that you're aware of these archangels and their missions, take a moment to choose an angel you might wish to call on. Maybe you want to connect to several angels. You can call on as many angels as you wish as frequently as you desire. They are waiting for you to connect, and they love to come to your aid. You don't need to physically see an angel or audibly hear them to know they are guiding you. Often you'll experience their guidance as a gut knowing or a strong intuitive guidance. Angels speak to you in many ways, so to understand their messages, pay attention to your feelings and intuition. Allow these relationships to benefit you, guide you, and bring you closer to the love of the Universe.

GUARDIAN ANGELS

Each of us has a guardian angel, who is devoted to our spiritual growth. Their mission is to serve, guide, and protect you while helping to further your growth on your spiritual path. Unlike archangels, your guardian angel works exclusively with you. They have unconditional love for you and are always by your side. Like archangels, guardian angels are always available to us, but they won't intervene in our lives unless we invite them of our free will or unless there is a life-threatening situation that occurs before it is our time to leave the body. Our guardian angels are always on call, ready to respond when we invite them in.

When you're struggling, call on your guardian angel for help. They are highly sensitive and can absorb your emotions to help you through difficult times. In the low moments of life, when we feel deep despair, we can often get the sense that there's a presence by our side—even if that sense is very subtle. That feeling is the presence of our guardian angels.

In one especially hard time in my life, I experienced a strong connection with my guardian angel, Peter. His presence is always with me, but I can feel him most when I'm struggling. In 2016, during a therapy session, I remembered childhood traumatic events from which I had dissociated. This moment of remembrance sent me into a deep state of depression. I was walking around retraumatized and terrified of the feelings I was experiencing. For several months I struggled to sleep, get out of bed, or even brush my teeth in the morning. I was disconnected from my spirit and my body. One night I couldn't sleep, and I went to the living room sofa so that I wouldn't disrupt my husband. Lying on the sofa, wide awake and shaken by my trauma, I burst into tears. I sobbed and wailed. The tears brought me relief and helped me break through my resistance. As I began to calm down, I felt as though I was lying in a warm embrace. I sensed strong arms holding me gently and a warm, loving energy surrounding me. Then I heard an inner voice reveal, "I am here with you, dear one." I knew instantly that this loving presence was my guardian angel, Peter. His arms surrounded me and gave me so much comfort and peace.

Guardian angels are our great protectors. Peter is always there for me when I need his protection and support. When I'm about to sit down at a book-signing table and greet hundreds of people, I ask Peter to stand beside me. I see him as my personal bodyguard and gatekeeper. He protects me so that I can sustain my energy throughout the signing. I never do anything challenging without inviting Peter to support me every step of the way.

FRIENDS FROM THE PAST

Spiritual guidance can also come from deceased friends from your past. In my early sober recovery, I had a dear friend named Lauren. She was a beautiful 26-year-old woman who'd been sober since she was 18. She was an amazing mentor to me in my recovery and embodied so much of what I wanted to attract in my own life. Lauren was studying to be a life coach, so she had hundreds of self-help books in her tiny NYC apartment. One afternoon Lauren went for a run in the park with her boyfriend and collapsed from a heart attack. That day we lost a human angel. Lauren's passing was deeply upsetting to me, but on a spiritual level, I knew that our relationship was not over. From the moment I heard the news of her death, I had no doubt she was going to be a great spiritual guide. I had a sense that her guidance was going to be especially helpful for young women trying to get sober or embark on a spiritual path. My intuition told me very clearly that she was going to help so many of us.

Her family generously offered that her close friends go to her apartment and save any items that would remind them of her. I was grateful for this. When I walked into her apartment, I noticed her bookshelf was still filled with the most incredible spiritual books. Almost every page was dog-eared and had notes written in the margins. She loved her books! I heard my intuition say, "Bring these books home and give them away to your coaching clients. And use them for your teachings." I trusted this guidance, so I packed up boxes of books and carried them down several flights of stairs to my home.

Lauren has always been a guide for me, especially early in my writing journey. I remember when I'd just sold my first book, *Add More ~ing to Your Life*. I was terrified because I didn't know yet how to write a book. I needed to learn structure, and outlining, and storytelling. I needed an editor to keep me on track. But I had no clue how to go about any of this. One night, lying awake and filled with fear about how I'd write an entire book, I prayed for spiritual guidance. I asked my guides to direct me toward the resources and support I needed to complete this first book. I knew I was on a mission, and I was willing to be guided to get the job done. After saying this prayer, I felt so much calmer knowing there was support on the way. My body and mind relaxed, and I fell asleep.

At 2 A.M. I abruptly woke up. I felt an inner call to get out of bed and walk to my bookshelf. At the time I was living in my studio apartment, and one of the walls was a huge built-in bookshelf packed with spiritual self-help books. Still half asleep, I felt my hand go directly to a book called *Living in the Light* by the author and spiritual teacher Shakti Gawain. I got back in bed and read the book from cover to cover! *Living in the Light* was the exact book I needed in order to understand how to write a spiritual self-help book. I loved how simply Shakti explained the principles and how easy it was to follow her outline. This book was the guidance that I needed to confidently begin writing my own book.

It probably won't come as a surprise to learn that the book had come from Lauren's collection! I know that it was Lauren who guided me to that book, and she continues to guide me today. I dedicated *Add More ~ing to Your Life* to Lauren because I knew that her guidance had been instrumental in helping me accomplish my first big literary endeavor.

GUIDANCE FROM YOUR FAMILY

One of my most cherished guides is my grandmother Fritzie. My grammy passed away at the age of 93 following complications that resulted from a bad fall. The weeks leading up to her death were a real challenge because, while she had all her mental faculties, her body was failing. After Grammy's accident, my mother and I had to decide whether the doctor should operate on her injured shoulder or let her live on medication to anesthetize the pain. My mother and I spent two weeks agonizing over the problem. Grammy was a vibrant, sharp woman who never wanted to live on heavy medication. And it was clear that surgery would be a bad idea at her age.

Two weeks after Grammy's fall, I was preparing to lead a six-day workshop at a retreat center an hour away from my house. My team was waiting for me to put my bags in the car and get on the road. I excused myself and said, "I know it's not the ideal time, but I feel like I need to meditate." I sat down in my bedroom and began to meditate. Within moments I was lifted out of my body and entered another realm. My hands rose up in the air and my head tilted up toward the sky. I felt a powerful energy moving through my arms, as if I were sending someone on their way. I felt as though I was facilitating an important task. This was one of the deepest and most powerful meditations I've ever experienced.

After 10 minutes I felt my body release the energy and I centered back into my chair. Aware that I needed to leave, I got up to gather my things and hit the road. As I was about to walk out my door, my phone rang. It was my mother, and her voice was somber. She said, "Grammy just left her body a few minutes ago." I burst into tears of joy, grateful that I'd been there with her. I know that she called on me to help guide her as she released her physical body. I was also extremely happy that she had chosen to let go and not struggle in the physical form. I kept saying, "I'm so happy for her. I'm so happy for her."

This information was a lot to take in when I needed to head out to my training. In order to energetically prepare to lead my event, I knew I'd have to dedicate time to properly mourn once the training was over. I wanted to give my grandmother the respect and time that she deserved. Each day of my training, I held Grammy in the back of my mind. Through prayer I asked her to let me know that she had passed on safely, and I patiently awaited her message. The training ended, and on my way back home, I stopped at my friend Zoe's house. I sat at Zoe's dining table with another friend, Jenny, and we caught up. Zoe was excited to show off her new oracle deck, but an incoming call momentarily distracted me. While I was on the phone, Jenny picked a card for me. When I returned, the two sat silent as they shared with me the card that had been drawn. Depicted on it was an image of an elderly woman walking over a bridge. The caption read, "Grandmother ensures safe crossing." We all gazed at each other as tears rolled down our cheeks, feeling the profound clarity with which my Grammy was communicating. She had waited until I was ready to receive the message, and she had worked through Zoe and Jenny to make sure I got it!

This moment began a very genuine connection between my grandmother and me, one that has continued to strengthen over time. I always know that Grammy is right by my side and ready to step in whenever I need. I can sense her presence with me, and I constantly receive beautiful signs from her. I can hear her voice saying, "I love you, my darling."

You may have a close family member or friend who has passed on. Please let this story inspire you to begin a spiritual relationship with them. It's often devastating to our humanness when we lose a loved one. But there is deep relief when you embrace a spiritual relationship beyond your physical sight. Begin a dialogue with your loved one, and ask them to show you a sign that they are with you. You'll be amazed by the ways they show up. You may smell their perfume, be guided to their favorite book, or hear their name come through in a song. Pay attention to the guidance they send to you, and know that they are always by your side. Deceased loved ones and family members are some of our greatest guides. When we connect to them, they bridge our fearful thoughts back to love and help us live as Super Attractors. They guide us toward what we desire and what is of the highest good for our spiritual development. Let them in, and deepen your relationship through prayer, meditation, and daily conversation.

GUIDES CAN BE TEACHERS FROM YOUR PAST

One of my teacher guides is my late friend and mentor Dr. Wayne Dyer. In my meditations Wayne has been one of the clearest spirit guides. He swoops in and offers crystal-clear direction. He's also used me as a conduit for communicating with his daughters Serena, Saje, and Skye, with whom I'm friends.

When Wayne first started giving me messages to pass to his girls, I hesitated in contacting them. I questioned the messages and didn't want to offend them by suggesting I could hear guidance from their father. But Wayne was not going to let me be silent. One afternoon after channeling Wayne, I opened my Instagram to see a beautiful photo of him that his daughter Serena had posted. I knew the photo was a sign from Wayne that he was indeed connecting to me. So I commented on the photo and sent my love to Serena. An hour later I received a text from her saying, "That's so wild that you commented on my post. I've been thinking about you all day. I can't get you out of my mind!" I said, "I've been thinking of you too." But I made no mention of Wayne. An hour later I received a text message from a medium named Karen, who had been working with the Dyer family to connect them to Wayne. She said, "I need to talk to you." I barely knew Karen and was a little shocked by the urgency in her text, so I got on the phone with her right away. When we began speaking she said, "I don't know why, but I feel a strong urge to speak to you." I said, "Could it have something to do with Wayne? He's been coming through my meditations for weeks and he has so many messages for the girls. He keeps telling me that Serena is the voice box and needs to carry his message." She said, "That's it! I was channeling Wayne today and he said that Serena is the voice box." In this divine moment it became clear to me that Wayne was working through Karen to assure me that the messages I was receiving were indeed from him. As soon as I got off the phone with Karen, I got on a conference call with Skye and Serena to share this with them. I spent an hour channeling Wayne so he could offer them guidance through me. Wayne's presence is one of the most profound energies I can connect to and I'm deeply grateful for his guidance. Wayne has also made clear that he's available for anyone who wants to connect to love and light.

WELCOME YOUR GUIDES TO THE PARTY THAT IS YOU

If you haven't had experiences like these, I welcome you to keep an open mind. If you are willing to connect with your spirit guides, the steps below will start your relationship, keep you safe, enhance your life, and help you be a Super Attractor.

Being willing to connect with your spirit guides opens the door to guidance, but you want to be conscious not to leave the door wide open for any guide to step in. Think about it like this: You're throwing a party and you want only the most positive and loving people to show up. Therefore, you make a guest list and are sure not to invite anyone who doesn't support you. Similarly, welcoming your guides into your consciousness requires an invitation. If you're not clear about the type of guides you're willing to connect to, then it's possible to attract lower-vibration spiritual beings that do not serve your highest good. You decide who you want to invite to the party that is you. My medium mentors have taught me that the best way to begin connecting to our guides is to recite a prayer. One I commonly say is, *Thank you, guides of the highest truth and compassion, for revealing to me what I need to know.*

YOUR GUIDES ARE WAITING FOR YOUR REQUEST

It's important to reiterate that guides and angels can intervene in your life only when you ask for their help. Receiving spiritual guidance is dependent on your free will. And it's up to us whether or not we follow their guidance. My dear friend MaryAnn DiMarco, medium and author of *Believe, Ask, Act*, says, "Spirit guides open the door for us. It's our choice to walk through it or not."

A nice way to start is by introducing yourself to your guardian angel. Get comfortable in a private space where you won't be interrupted. Have a notebook by your side. Gently close your eyes and begin breathing long and deep. Silently send out the request to your guardian angel that you welcome them to reveal their name to you. Then begin any type of relaxation meditation that you use to get calm, centered, and connected to the Universe. (If you want my guidance with this meditation, visit GabbyBernstein.com/ SuperAttractor for my meditation for invoking your guardian angel.) Sit comfortably in your meditation for as long as you wish. In your meditation you may hear your guardian angel's name as an intuition, an audible sound, or a guidance to write it down in your journal. If for some reason you don't receive the name in your meditation, trust that it's coming. You may find that hours later a name will come through a song or a billboard or in some other unexpected way. There are many ways that your guide can reveal their name. Trust that when you receive it, you'll intuitively know it's them. Don't question the name you receive, even if it sounds strange to you. And don't be surprised if you begin to feel their presence around you. They're so excited that you welcomed them in that they may want to make their presence known. This is the beginning of a beautiful and supportive relationship that will guide you for a lifetime.

CONNECTING TO YOUR GUIDES

Once you have been introduced to your guides, there are many ways that you can ask them for help. One of the easiest is to simply send out a silent request for support. For instance, if you're caught up in fearful thoughts, you can say, "Thank you, guides of the highest truth and compassion, for helping me heal this fear and return to love." Or if you want to be more specific and work with a certain angel guide, you can say, "Thank you, Archangel Michael, for helping me through this scary situation. I welcome your protection and guidance." Or if you're consciously connected to your very own guardian angel, you can call on the angel directly. These gentle requests are the same as a prayer. Your prayers are intentions to receive support. Trust that your positive intent is enough to reveal profound spiritual guidance. I like to begin these prayers with the words "thank you" because they remind me that guidance is already on the way.

I have found it very powerful to connect to my guides through writing. I often sit in a silent meditation with my journal by my side. Before I begin my meditation, I write my intention at the top of the page. I write, *Thank you, guides of the highest truth and compassion, for providing me clear direction with* _____. I ask them for support with my health, marriage, business, or anything I desire. Then I gently lead myself into a silent meditation practice. At the point in my meditation when I notice a nudge from my guides, I pick up my pen and begin to freewrite. I let my pen flow, and I don't edit anything. In just a few moments, the most beautiful and insightful words come through. Words and ideas that are not mine stream onto the page. I'm often blown away by some of the guidance I receive.

If you're new to freewriting, you may have a range of experiences when you begin. You might start channeling right away, or it may take you some time to become comfortable with this practice. Just let your pen flow, and don't edit. Write down whatever comes forth, even if it seems mundane or weird at first. Have faith in the process, and allow it to unfold in whatever way it does.

YOUR GUIDES WILL HELP YOU IN MANY WAYS

Asking your guides for help gives them the freedom to help you more. As with any relationship, the more you nurture it, the more it can grow. As soon as you welcome your guides' presence, you will feel your thoughts and energy begin to return to alignment with the love of the Universe. Your guides will remind you that you are love and that the voice of your Higher Self is your only true voice. They will give you clear direction when you feel misguided, and they will always lead you to solutions of the highest good for all.

In the coming chapter, I will help you get into the habit of surrendering your obstacles to your guides so that you no longer have to rely on your own strength. When you accept the guidance of your Higher Self, angels, spirit guides, or even deceased family members, you will feel a sense of support you've never known before. *A Course in Miracles* says, "The presence of fear is a sure sign that you are trusting in your own strength." When we learn to stop trusting only in our own strength and to rely instead on the spiritual realm and our Higher Selves, we can live with ease and grace, and we can truly be Super Attractors.

Chapter 7

DO LESS AND ATTRACT MORE

In spring 2017, around the time that I began channeling Wayne Dyer, I received more confirmation that he was indeed connecting with me. I had a private reading with my medium friend Rebecca Rosen. In the middle of the reading, she said, "Your guru is connecting to you. It's your teacher. It's Wayne!" She went on to confirm that the messages I was receiving were from him, and she assured me that I should trust my ability to connect to his guidance. Then she told me that he would be a great source of support for me when I was speaking publicly. She suggested that I call on him before every talk and that I'd immediately feel a sense of calm come over me. I loved receiving this guidance, and I looked forward to welcoming Wayne to support my next talk.

Later that month I gave one of the biggest talks of my life. I was invited to speak at Oprah's SuperSoul Sessions and lead a talk called "The Universe Has Your Back." In this talk I planned to share a very vulnerable story, and I was nervous about it. (Not to mention the fact that my ego was going wild with the idea that it was Oprah's event.) I'd made Oprah very special, and I was putting a lot of emphasis on the importance of this talk. At this stage in my speaking career, I had stopped getting nervous, but in this instance my ego's projections were making me uncomfortable.

I was very anxious the morning of my talk. I knew that my ego was in the way of my Super Attractor power. In a moment of inner crisis, I remembered Rebecca's suggestion to call on Wayne to work through me. So I sat on my hotel bed and meditated. In my meditation I invited Wayne to enter into my mind and guide me. Within seconds I could feel the most calming presence come over me. I felt almost instant relief. It was as though his energy was incorporating into mine, and I was able to embody great peace. My anxiety lifted, and I was in a perfect state of grace. I opened my eyes and felt ready to show up for my talk with my Higher Self speaking through me.

An hour later I pulled into the parking lot near the backstage entrance of the venue. There was a large SUV in front of my car. I got out of the car, and as the Universe would have it, Ms. Winfrey was getting out of her SUV at the exact same time. Had I still been stuck in my ego, I probably would've bumbled my way through an interaction. But with Wayne by my side, I was able to see her as an equal and greet her with grace. We hugged and talked about how excited we were for the day.

The hours leading up to my talk were relaxed and easy. The moment before I stepped onto the stage, I invited Wayne to come with me. I felt his presence on the stage with me that day. The words I spoke were effortless. I was able to release my ego's projections of being on Oprah's stage, and I stopped making my talk about me. Rather, I was able to make it about service and love. I taught from my heart. Wayne's guidance got me out of the way and helped me rely on a humility and strength beyond my own. The talk has since been shared on YouTube to viewers throughout the world and has hopefully helped many people learn the spiritual practice of surrender. Wayne's energy is infused in every replay.

Spirit guides help us to get out of our own way and to stop relying on our own strength. They are always guiding us to connect to our Super Attractor energy and allow the flow of love to move through everything we do. As Wayne would say, "When you are in spirit, you are inspired!"

Being a Super Attractor is about strengthening your faith, tuning in to the energy of love, and allowing the Universe to guide you. To begin the practice of allowing, we must get out of the way and let spirit give us direction.

In the last chapter, I introduced you to the kinds of spirit guides you can connect to. In the coming pages, I'll expand on those lessons, teaching you how to regularly turn over your desires to the care of the Universe or a spiritual guidance of your own understanding. The daily practice of releasing your plans to spirit will help you cultivate your ability to be still and embrace the present moment. In stillness you will receive. Establishing a strong spiritual connection will help you release anxiety and feel a sense of immense relief. You'll stop pouring all your mental, emotional, and even physical effort into pushing, controlling, and trying to make things happen. Instead, you will be guided.

I want to give you the experience of connecting to your very own guides. I want you to feel the freedom of releasing control and allowing a presence beyond your own to lead the way. And I want you to feel even more connected to your Super Attractor power. When you follow these steps, spirit will show up quickly.

STOP RELYING ON YOUR OWN STRENGTH

We've grown accustomed to the belief that our will is what makes things happen. But the secret to feeling good and manifesting our desires without struggling and suffering is to stop relying on our own strength! We do this by welcoming the power of spirit, the Universal energy of love, to lead our thoughts and actions. Think of this as a collaboration between you and the Universe. You no longer have to feel solely responsible for figuring out life, making all major decisions, and taking action on your dreams. There is a force of love within you and around you supporting your every move. The way to access this force is to simply get out of the way. As long as you're relying on your will, your plans, and your timeline, you'll feel blocked and fearful—stressed in the present, worried about the future, unsure of decisions, and so on. But the moment you let go and allow, an energy of support will take over.

Welcoming this powerful force of spiritual connection into your life can be confusing to your ego. We frequently rely on fear to feel a false sense of safety and control, when in truth that fear is what manifests more uncertainty, pain, and suffering. It's easy to fall into fearful patterns from childhood or past experiences and feel paralyzed by them. When we're triggered by fear, we can revert to a childlike part of ourselves that will do anything to feel safe and in charge of things. Many people live on the edge of a fight-or-flight state, falling into it whenever their egos sound the alarm. But imagine how wonderful it would be to surrender that part of yourself to the care of a higher power. What would your life be like if you stopped thinking you had to protect yourself or take care of everything in order to move your life forward? How different would you be if you knew that you could surrender your life to a presence of support-ive guidance?

The clearest path to this freedom is to get into the habit of relying on spiritual guidance and the energy of the Uni-verse. Consistently turning to angels, spirit guides, your Higher Self, and the wisdom of the Universe will lead you to what is of the highest good for all. Learning to rely on spiritual strength will give you incredible freedom. In order to establish or strengthen your connection to the spiritual realm, you must step out of the way.

To begin to surrender to the loving guidance that is always available to you, start by invoking the guidance that you want to connect to.

You may feel most comfortable connecting to your Higher Self (inner wisdom) or to the love of the Universe (or God). Or you may be inspired by the archangels and choose to connect to a specific angel who can help you with your particular situation. Maybe you like the idea of connecting to a deceased loved one whom you've missed. If you're not immediately clear about who you want to connect to, take a moment to review the guides in Chapter 6 and see what inspires you. When my editor Katie read Chapter 6, she immediately knew that Archangel Ariel was her guide. She felt an instant connection to Ariel because she's the guide for animal lovers and environmentalists. Don't question your intuition when it comes to connecting to guides. Whichever guide comes to your mind immediately is who you're meant to connect to. Remember, they're waiting for your call.

CONNECTING TO THE ENERGY OF SPIRIT

Loving support can come in different frequencies, and the clearer you are about the spiritual guidance you want to receive, the more familiar you will become with the energy of the guidance you're connecting to. For instance, when I ask to connect to Archangel Michael, known as the archangel of protection, I sense the energy in the room expand, and I feel protected. When I call on Wayne for support, I feel a beautiful sense of peace and calm. When I ask my Higher Self to align me with my inner wisdom, I feel a speedy and excited energy, as though I'm being prepared for new information to come through. There are many different energetic frequencies, and it's powerful to learn the different forms of guidance that come from each one.

Guides will use symbols and signs to let you know they're there. You may have a religious connection to an ascended master such as Jesus, Buddha, or Mother Mary, who regularly shows you a symbol of their presence. Or maybe you have a spiritual bond with a deceased family member who connects to you through a specific sign such as a song, a fragrance, or an image. Guides will be creative and clear when they show up. You may be blown away by how clear they are. Let yourself be in awe of the magnificent guidance that's available to you.

It doesn't matter which guide you connect to. Trust that your intuition is leading you to the guidance that will resonate with you most. The same way you may feel aligned with a specific yoga teacher or professor, you may feel a connection to a particular spiritual guide. You can have many different types of spiritual guides or regularly connect to just one. It doesn't matter how you're guided; what matters is that you surrender your will to the support of a loving presence of power beyond your own. Each form of spiritual guidance has the same purpose: to lead you back to love.

Choose the guide you want to connect with now. Open your journal and write down the first name that comes to mind. It doesn't matter whether it's an archangel, a deceased family member, your Higher Self (inner guidance system), or any other spirit guide. Don't think too much—just write down the type of guidance you're inspired to connect to.

Now that you've clarified the guidance that you want to connect to, it's time to tune in to that energetic frequency. As a reminder, each guide has their own energy, and the more often you connect to them, the easier it will be to know who you're with.

TUNE IN THROUGH PRAYER

When you're stuck in your logical and practical thought system, you can't connect to the infinite wisdom that is available to you at all times. But when you pray, you temporarily suspend the limitations of your worldly mind and reconnect to the infinite wisdom of a divine guidance beyond your own. Prayer is the pathway to surrender. When you pray for guidance, you release your control, your will, and your agenda to the care of your spiritual guide. Prayer is a bridge from your controlling, fearful mind to the right mind of love. Whenever you pray for guidance, you instantly realign with your Super Attractor power. A prayer reclaims your faith in a higher power and is a humble request to transcend the false, fear-based beliefs of the world and remember the light of who you are. When praying becomes second nature, you feel relief because you know that at any time you can connect to the love of the Universe through the spiritual guidance that is always available to you. Of course, fearful thoughts will come up, but you'll replace them with a prayer. Let prayer become a habit that is stronger than your fear.

The first prayer we'll practice is a prayer to connect. This prayer can open the door to receiving spiritual guidance. Sit comfortably in a private space with your Super Attractor journal by your side. Then say this prayer silently or out loud:

Thank you, guide of the highest truth and compassion, [name the guide you're connecting to], for revealing your presence to me. I welcome you now.

Take a deep breath in, then release.

Continue to breathe deeply as you allow your guide's presence to enter your space.

Following your prayer, pay attention to how you feel. Did the energy in the room shift? Did you feel lighter, tingly, calm, inspired, or protected? Did you have an intuitive thought? Pick up your journal and document what the guidance felt like to you. Don't question any of the feelings that came through. When you connect to any kind of guide, you're aligning with an energy field beyond the physical realm. This energy will likely feel different from what you've grown accustomed to. Don't judge it, and don't be afraid of it. Remember: You tuned in to the energy of the highest good. As long as you've made that clear distinction, you can attract only high, loving energy.

If you didn't feel any guidance right away, be patient. Sometimes guidance can show up later on. Maybe you'll see a sign you asked for, or you'll have a dream with clear direction, or maybe you'll sense a presence by your side when you fall asleep. Don't rush the connection.

Once you've felt a connection to the spiritual realm, you've opened the door to receive divine guidance, clear direction, and great wisdom. Now you will use meditation to slow down and listen to the guidance that is available to you. In peaceful stillness spirit can connect to you. In prayer you ask for guidance, and in meditation you listen.

A meditation for spiritual guidance

Follow this meditative breath practice and attune your energy to the guidance that is available to you now. (You can listen to the guided meditation on the resources page at GabbyBernstein.com/SuperAttractor.) After your short meditation, pick up your journal and let the guidance pour onto the page.

Begin by slowing down your breath so that you can tune your energy to the frequency of the guidance that is available to you now.

Breathe in through your nose for a count of four.

Hold your breath for a count of four.

Release your breath through your mouth for a count of four.

Practice this cycle of breath three more times.

Then continue to breathe long and deep for one more minute. On the inhale extend your diaphragm, and on the exhale let it relax. Inhale, extending your diaphragm, and on the exhale, release. This breath pattern will ensure that you inhale and exhale completely.

Set the intention to align your energy with the supportive guidance that is surrounding you now.

Once you feel your energy shift to a peaceful, calm, inspired frequency, pick up your journal and write this sentence at the top of the page:

Thank you, guidance of the highest truth and compassion [you can name your guide here if you wish], for showing me what you want me to know.

(Feel free to be more specific by asking them to reveal to you how to handle a certain situation, etc.)

For five minutes or more, let your pen flow onto the page. Don't edit anything. Just let it flow.

LET GUIDANCE FLOW

Wayne Dyer said, "When you remember to stay in-spirit you'll realize that when one thing appears to be going wrong, you can see clearly ten things that are going right." As soon as you align your thoughts and energy with a loving guide, you will be given clear direction, creative solutions, radical inspiration, peace—and so much more. Guidance comes in many forms. Pay attention to everything and dismiss nothing.

Upon establishing your spiritual connection through this process, you may notice that people respond to your energy differently. Experiences that used to stress you out may be easier to navigate. Wild synchronicities may show up in your life. You might even feel as though the presence of spirit is always by your side. Each time you choose to tune in to spirit, guidance of the highest truth will show up for you.

Over the next week, continue to practice your prayer, meditation, and journaling exercise. Then document the connections and guidance you receive. Take notes in your journal throughout the day, and pay close attention to each sign of guidance. These three steps will make spiritual guidance easy to access and strengthen your connection to it. For the next week, practice these three steps each morning:

1. Tune in through prayer and invoke the presence of your guide.
2. Relax and receive guidance through meditation.
3. Document the guidance you receive.

The more time you devote to these methods, the more undeniable the presence of spirit will become. When you consciously choose to align with the presence of spirit, you will notice incredible shifts occur in your energy, your experiences, and the people you encounter in everyday life. Your ego will want to resist it at all costs, saying things like "This is just a coincidence" or "That would have happened anyway." Your consistency can combat this ego backlash. When you consistently welcome spirit into your consciousness, you commit to a deeper connection with the guidance around you. Pay attention to the divine guidance you receive, and let spirit show you what to do.

RELY ON A HIGHER POWER

Living a Super Attractor life means that we learn to rely on a higher power. Each time we rely on our own strength and turn our back on spirit, we weaken our connection to the Universe and to our Super Attractor power. Relying on a higher power keeps us connected to the spiritual realm and to infinite possibilities, synchronicity, and joy. Being guided doesn't mean that we give up our own decision-making ability, but it does mean that decisions come more easily. We feel clear and directed rather than uncertain and hesitant. When we encounter obstacles, we know where to turn for help, and we receive divine direction. Relying on a higher power adds richness to your life because you no longer feel pressured to figure everything out. You can let go and allow.

The Universal energy of love is within you, but often you need help connecting to it. Let the Universe and your guides be your constant bridge back to love, strength, and clear direction.

Don't be afraid to ask for spiritual guidance in any situation. When you're at the doctor's office, ask spirit to work through the healthcare provider. When you're in a job interview, invite spirit to speak through you with confidence. Or when you're arguing with a friend, ask spirit to intervene and help you find forgiveness and solutions. There is nothing you cannot surrender. And most of all, trust in the guidance around you all the time—not just when it seems convenient, but all the time. I want you to make relying on spirit your daily habit. The more you lean on spirit, the more you will be led.

DO LESS AND ATTRACT MORE

Trust that your alignment with the Universe is enough to co-create the world you want to see. Lesson 38 of *A Course in Miracles* teaches, "There is nothing my holiness cannot do." When you surrender your will to the care of spirit and the Universe, you attune your energy to an ever-present stream of well-being. In this surrendered state, you accept your holiness, and there's nothing you cannot do. Accepting your holiness means you have strong faith in the Universe and spiritual guidance. Your faith makes attracting second nature. In this space of faith, you allow the Universe to flow, and you can do less and attract more.

LET SPIRIT TAKE THE WHEEL

Many people live with the mistaken belief that they must control in order to attract. We are all controlling in our own ways (even if we don't identify as such). But the Universe doesn't respond to controlling energy. The Universe responds when we let go and welcome divine guidance. When there is a controlling energy behind your actions, you won't receive the outcome you truly want. The key to attracting your desires is to release them.

Letting go offers us all we want, but doing it can feel tricky. Your fear resists it stubbornly. One thing to expect is that some areas of your life may be easier to turn over to spirit, while others are harder. This is normal. For example, you may find it easy to rely on spirit in your career but discover that you resist it in your relationships. It helps to begin practicing connecting to your guides and surrendering in the areas where you're more detached—where things don't feel so "high stakes" and you have a more relaxed attitude toward the outcome. In time it will become easier to release your bigger attachments. Get into this habit by surrendering something that you're less attached to. Practice letting spirit support you in an area of your life where it's easy for you to receive. This way you can begin to create spiritual proof that you are indeed guided. That spiritual proof will give you faith that the Universe has your back and that it's safe to let go. Each moment of faith adds up. With your new-found faith, you'll be inspired to turn over more and more areas of your life to the care of a higher power of your own understanding.

A spiritual connection is a habit that requires that you rely on a higher power rather than your own will. So surrender the small stuff as well as the big stuff. Ask spirit for help with your meal prep just as you would with a medical problem. There is no request too big or small. The spiritual realm is waiting for you to ask and receive. Turn it all over to the Universe, and expect divine guidance.

When you rely on a higher power, you cultivate the ability to be still and embrace the present moment. This frees you from spending time or mental effort worrying about how things are going. You'll no longer obsess about the future or feel unsettled about what's not yet happening. You will feel faithful regardless of the circumstances. When we cultivate a connection to spirit, we can trust in the Universe no matter what.

BELIEVING IN A HIGHER POWER

Belief is a prerequisite to becoming a Super Attractor. Each time we surrender our will to spirit, we deepen our belief in a power greater than ourselves. I don't expect you to transcend your fear and believe in spiritual guidance right away. My hope is that you will continue to connect to spiritual guidance regularly to strengthen your belief every day. Say a prayer, meditate on the energy of love, suspend your disbelief for one minute, and feel your way into faith one step at a time. There is so much relief in knowing that there is a power greater than you guiding you every step of the way.

When we believe in a higher power, we can stop worrying, controlling, and obsessing over the how, when, or why. We can get out of the way and allow spirit to guide us. We can let others help us, let intuition flow, and create from a place of inspiration. Believing in spiritual guidance gives us certainty and the freedom to keep dreaming even when we can't yet see the result. If you're waiting for a result, it's spirit that gives you peace in the interim. When what you desire feels far from reach, it's spirit that gives you direction and the inspiration to move forward. Freedom, peace, and joy come from living in-spirit. And it begins with your willingness to let go.

Part of living in union with your spirit guides is trusting that you are worthy of the love of the Universe. We tend to resist our spiritual connection because deep down we don't believe we're worthy of support and unconditional love. We think we have to be the creator, and we forget that we come from an ever-present energy of love that created us. Living in connection to spirit means that we remember that we are one with this energy of love and that there's nothing we cannot do when we're aligned with the Universe. My prayer is that these concepts become more than just words you read in spiritual books. My prayer is that they become truths that you know on a deep level. You deserve to know your magnificence, feel supported, and live with ease. Miracles are your birthright. It's time to remember.

I encourage you to let yourself off the hook and have some fun with the practices in this chapter. This is an opportunity to try out a new behavior pattern, so treat it as an adventure! It will become easier and easier to let go when you let yourself enjoy the process of being guided. With your trust in your spirit guides, you can rest easy knowing that you are being led every step of the way.

It feels so exciting to write these lessons. Each word I write is a reminder of the support that's available to us at all times. I have big visions for how this book will support you. I have faith in a powerful plan beyond my own because I can feel the free-flowing creative energy of spiritual guidance and love moving through my hands as I type these words. This is spiritual connection and manifestation in action. Right here, right now.

With your connection to spirit, anything is possible. In Chapter 8 you will tap into your guides and the energy of the Universe so you can take the next steps in co-creating your desires. I'll teach you my Spiritually Aligned Action Method, which will give you confidence in the steps you take toward your desires. Get psyched for what's to come, and invite spirit to continue this journey with you.

Chapter 8

TAKING SPIRITUALLY ALIGNED ACTION

In 2008 I was just a few years into my career as a life coach and motivational speaker. I was living in New York City and hosting lectures at hotels, yoga studios, and community centers. I led group coaching workshops in my apartment, and I was preaching to anyone who would listen. I was on a mission to spread my message to the masses.

At this time, I felt a new zeitgeist emerging. It seemed as if more women, especially, were turning to spirituality instead of shoe boutiques in the quest for happiness. Lots of people were becoming health-conscious, trading cocktails and clubs for green juice and yoga. All over the world, I could see spiritual seekers longing for permission to wake up. In them, I recognized myself when I was first setting off on my spiritual path. They were looking for a community of like-minded people. They wanted guidance on how to open up to a spiritual connection. I felt that it was my responsibility to let them know that they were not alone. I wanted to tell them it was hip to be spiritual and that they could be free to explore new beliefs!

I so strongly believed in sharing my message with a bigger audience that I decided to apply my PR savvy to get the word out about what I saw happening. One afternoon I had an inspired idea and burst out, "There's a new movement of life coaches and spiritual seekers. I'm going to pitch a story about it to the *New York Times* Sunday Styles section!"

This had seemingly come out of nowhere, and my intern looked at me with a confused expression. But I was inspired, faithful, and confident. I had listened to the divine guidance I received, and I knew it was time to act on it. I grabbed the number of a reporter I knew who wrote for the Styles section and dialed immediately.

To my surprise, he answered.

"This is Allen."

"Hey, Allen, it's Gabby Bernstein," I said. "We met a while back at a dinner in Soho. I'm calling because I have a neat story for you."

Allen said, "Tell me quickly. I don't have a lot of time."

"Got it," I said. "The pitch is something like this: All the girls who used to want to be Carrie Bradshaw now want to be more like self-help author Wayne Dyer. There's a new movement, and I can give you a full story on this trend."

"Interesting. I'll get back to you."

His tone was just a little snarky . . . but his interest was all I needed. The seed was planted, and I released my pitch to the Universe. Intuitively I knew there was something awesome to come.

Nearly nine months went by with very little response from Allen. He'd check in from time to time to see what I was up to and let me know that there was still interest in the story. I remained patient and faithful, and I trusted that my powerful intentions combined with my faith were enough to allow my vision for this story to become my reality. I let it go and allowed the Universe to do her thing. Instead of obsessing over each email or trying to force anything, I turned over my goal to the care of the Universe. I knew that everything would unfold exactly as it should. I focused instead on being of service every day, on spreading my message and helping more people discover and strengthen their spiritual connections. *A Course in Miracles* says, "Those who are certain of the outcome can afford to wait, and wait without anxiety." I was certain that whatever happened would be of the highest good, which made it easy to be patient.

I received no real response about my pitch until the fall of 2009, when Allen called me out of the blue. He said, "Gabby, it's Allen. The *Times* has picked up your story. I have a week to interview, do a photoshoot, check out your group coaching, and write the piece. Let's get on it!"

My story was coming to life! Within 24 hours I had scheduled the photoshoot and set up my interview with Allen.

At 9 P.M. that Wednesday, Allen came to my little studio apartment to sit in on my group coaching session, surrounded by eager young women meditating and praying. Afterward, he stuck around to interview me so he could get a better sense of my work. We sat on the futon couch, behind which hung a huge vision board that spanned the entire wall. This board held the pictures I had collected to represent all the dreams I had for my life: a loving couple holding hands, engagement rings, inspirational quotes, and white sand beaches.

In the bottom right-hand corner, I'd pinned up a masthead from the *New York Times* Sunday Styles section. Allen pointed at the masthead and said, "What's this?" I explained that I'd been manifesting this story for a while. Three years earlier I'd seen a feature in the Styles section about some food blogger friends of mine. While reading the piece, I'd thought about how I wanted that type of story for my own work. So I'd ripped out the masthead and put it on my vision board. It had been pinned there for three years.

Allen looked shocked. He turned to me and said, "I wrote that story about the food bloggers! That masthead is from the piece that I wrote three years ago. And now, three years later, I'm writing your cover story for the Styles section. Wow, I guess all this spiritual stuff works."

In that moment I smiled as I received a little wink from the Universe. This synchronicity was a sure sign that I had surrendered to the natural laws of manifesting and allowed the Universe to have my back as I co-created my reality.

Thankfully I didn't try to control this manifestation but instead allowed it to come into form naturally. That cover story was a major catalyst for my career and helped me fulfill my vision of sharing spirituality with a broader audience. My patience, certainty, and faith cleared space for the Universe, guides, and angels to deliver. Spirit works through people to support your great work in the world. When you follow your intuition and inspiration, you can be sure spirit is guiding you. I know that many spirits worked through Allen to make this happen.

The story is a nice example of how we can effortlessly co-create with the Universe when we merge our actions with inspiration. Without realizing it at the time, I had applied a specific method to manifest my vision into reality. Today I refer to it as the Spiritually Aligned Action Method. When you apply this method to anything you desire, you can trust that you're co-creating with the Universe rather than forcing a vision into form.

The Spiritually Aligned Action Method is a practice that requires inspiration and faith in spirit. When we merge our desire with our faith, we can take action from a place of peace rather than control. It's this presence of peace that allows the Universe to support us fully. By taking spiritually aligned action, we can trust that an energy beyond our own is working on our behalf and that everything is working out for us—even if we don't know exactly when or how it will happen. This method will help you attune your energy to that peaceful, inspired presence so that everything you do will be backed with your Super Attractor power. Follow these steps and practice them regularly to see how supportive the Universe can be when you take spiritually aligned action!

MY SPIRITUALLY ALIGNED ACTION METHOD

Step 1: Make sure your desire is backed by inspiration and service

My desire to have a cover story in the *New York Times* Sunday Styles section was backed with service. I knew the story would help new seekers feel less alone, heal their fearful perceptions, and become a support system to other people seeking solutions. I was greatly inspired by this desire to serve. I deeply understood what it felt like to be a new spiritual seeker, and I wanted others like me to never feel alone. The sense of belonging was what I had longed for when I started out on my own spiritual path. With clear service and inspiration behind my wish to be in the *Times*, I removed all disbelief. I stayed committed to my manifestation by sticking to high-vibe thoughts of how this story would help readers seeking a spiritual awakening of their own.

When the desire you're manifesting is aligned with service and inspiration, it is invincible. Because my primary intention was to help spread the message of spiritual awareness to new seekers, the process was backed with an unstoppable force of inspiration. It wasn't about feeding my ego. Instead, I wanted to help wake up a new generation of seekers. I learned a clear and lasting lesson from this experience: true manifestations are powered by service and inspiration.

You may be thinking, "How do I know if my desire is backed with service and inspiration?" You may also be thinking, "What if what I want isn't about changing the world? What if I want to find love or get out of debt? How is that of service to others?" It's important to understand that if your desire brings you joy, then it's backed with inspiration. And as long as your desire is in the pursuit of the highest good for all, you can trust it will be supported by spirit. Your sincere joy and desire to serve bring more light to the world. But it's equally important to tune in to *why* you want something and understand what energy is behind it. There are times when we really want something because it will make us feel better or more special than others. Other times we desire something because we hope it will mask one of our core wounds and help us avoid healing it. For instance, maybe you want a promotion at work so your family will approve of you. Or maybe you want to buy something expensive just so you can show off to friends. Or maybe you want a relationship because you don't feel complete on your own and are scared of being single. These example desires are backed by neediness and fear. They don't feel inspired or service oriented because they're filled with a need for external validation or completion rather than inner peace. Check in with yourself about any ego-driven desires that may be present. It's wonderful to be unapologetic about what you want, but always pay attention to the energy that backs up your desire.

One simple way to clear up the energy behind your desire is to ask yourself, "Does this desire make me feel inspired and serve others?" Take a moment to write in your journal about how your desire lights you up. Then take it even further, and write about how your inspiration and positive energy serves others. Let your pen flow, and write your way into powerful alignment. When you align your energy with this service and inspiration, you can trust that it will propel your vision forward. Try writing for at least five minutes in your journal, and then read over what you wrote. Let yourself feel into the feelings of joy, inspiration, and great contribution. Give yourself permission to celebrate your desires.

Step 2: Believe the Universe will deliver

Because I felt so inspired and connected to the service behind my desire, it was easy to believe that the Universe had my back. I knew that there was an audience for my work, and I knew it needed to get out to the world. When I reflected on how much my spiritual teachers had served me on my path, I knew that I could do the same for a new generation of seekers. I was so lit up by my desire that I unapologetically claimed my vision of getting my work in front of the people who needed it most. When we're spiritually aligned with our desires, we can have faith that the Universe is co-creating with us.

I also had a lot of clarity behind my desire. I knew that this story needed to be in the *New York Times* Sunday Styles section because that's where my reader was. She was looking for happiness in the next fashion trend, and I saw a beautiful opportunity to meet her where she was and remind her of what she truly wanted most: a spiritual life. But I didn't limit my belief. I trusted that it would be *The New York Times* or something better. When claiming your desire, it's important to state clearly what you want and then surrender it by adding, "This or something better." This way you stay open to the creative guidance from the Universe and don't limit your manifesting power. Often the Universe has a plan that's better than your own!

The more you believe in the support of the Universe, the more you will receive. You can accept that manifesting is a collaborative process and that spirit will lead the way when you're inspired. I believed in the vision because it made me feel good. The strength of my belief is what gave me the inner power to pick up the phone and call Allen in the first place. Belief comes when you feel unapologetic about your desires and unafraid to claim them. By praying and meditating daily, I stayed connected to the spirit and service behind my desire. Maintaining this connection allowed me to stay committed to my vision, even when Allen was silent for months.

Your ego may resist the concept of believing in the guidance of the Universe. When you notice this resistance, go back to your journal and read what you wrote about how your desire brings you joy and serves the world. The more you align your thoughts and energy with the joy and service of your desire, the more you'll believe that the Universe has your back.

Step 3: Take action from a place of spiritual alignment

With inspiration, service, and belief, you're ready to take action. You'll know you're taking spiritually aligned action because it will feel almost effortless. You won't second-guess yourself or ask for the opinions of others. You'll feel connected to every move you make. Every action will be backed with genuine confidence and fearlessness. There will be no resistance in your way.

I was in a clear state of spiritual alignment when I fearlessly picked up the phone to pitch *The New York Times*. My high vibes and confidence came through the phone line. Had I lacked spiritual alignment in that moment, Allen would have hung up before I even delivered the pitch. Spiritual alignment is what put this manifestation into motion.

Taking action from a spiritually aligned place is an awesome feeling. You don't question yourself, you're upbeat, and you know you're on the right track. It doesn't even matter how others respond because your alignment is enough to keep positive momentum flowing through your desires. The Universe will quickly reflect your alignment back to you. The next steps will unfold naturally. Whatever action you take from spiritual alignment will be greatly supported.

Step 4: Have patience

Thanks to my patience, I didn't push Allen to write the story. Had I done that, I probably would've pissed him off and deflected the opportunity. Instead I settled into my strong belief and allowed the story to come out at the perfect time. The piece landed one month before my first book, *Add More ~ing to Your Life*, was set to release and right before I headed off on a book tour. This publicity helped open countless doors for me from that point on. Patience and faith in the Universal timing allowed the manifestation to happen at the perfect time.

It's important to understand how patience is a great virtue when it comes to attracting your desires. When you connect to the feeling of knowing that whatever is of the highest good is coming to you, then you can relax and trust it's on the way. If you're reading this, thinking, "I'm totally screwed! Patience is not my strong suit," then I want to reassure you that you can cultivate patience by following the first three steps in this method. When you merge inspiration, service, and belief, you can trust that you're aligned with spirit and are being guided to the highest good for all. Get yourself into an excited state, dream big, and don't be afraid to believe in your visions. When you do this, patience will come naturally.

MANIFESTING IS AN ART

The Spiritually Aligned Action Method will help you access a creative force within. As with any creative project, we must hone our skills and allow inspiration to move through us. When we embody this creative force, life gets really fun. But it's important to know that manifesting isn't about having total control or satisfying all our short-term desires. True manifesting isn't even about getting what we think we want. It's about receiving what is of the highest good for all. Yes, you will have experiences in which you'll attract an outcome that is exactly as you projected. But controlling outcomes to get just what you want isn't the goal. Remember, your plan is not always the best plan! When you surrender to the art of manifesting, you can trust that spirit is guiding you toward your desires and much more.

Manifesting is the creative process of aligning with the energy of the Universe to co-create an experience that elevates your spirit and the spirit of the world. Manifesting isn't about getting; it's about becoming. The more you let go, the more you become a match for what you desire. Remember that your energy attracts its likeness. Following the Spiritually Aligned Action Method will help you get out of the way and let the Universe support you. You'll no longer feel stuck, blocked, or powerless. Instead, you'll harness the creative forces within you and take powerful actions from that place of Super Attractor power. The positive, faithful energy that you embody will be a reflection of the energy of the Universe. In a state of positive flow, the Universe matches your vibrational frequency and aligns you with your desires. When you're spiritually aligned, listening to the voice of your inner wisdom and allowing the love of the Universe to lead you, you're in a state of faith rather than fear. When you follow the Spiritually Aligned Action Method, you allow the Universe to guide you to what is of the highest good.

LET'S TRY THE METHOD NOW

To start, take an honest inventory of how you may be praying for what you think you need. In what ways are you controlling your actions to try to force an outcome? Are you trying different tactics to turn your romantic partner into someone they're not? Are you pushing to get your work seen on social media? Look at the ways in which your actions are backed with fear rather than faith. Start paying regular attention to how your controlling requests to the Universe may be blocking you from receiving what is of the highest good.

It's safe to get honest about the ways you block the flow of the Universe. We must look at our egos in order to bring them to the light. There are countless instances in my own life when I've tried to control rather than surrender. I tried to control the timing of my conception and the outcome of a book launch, and I spent my twenties trying to control every romantic partner in order to feel safe. I'm not ashamed of the ways I detoured into fear. I'm proud that I can see these misaligned moments as opportunities to witness my disconnect from the Universe. The sooner you look at the ways you're trying to control the Universe, the sooner you can surrender.

Make a list in your journal of all the ways you're controlling your desires.

Once you're clear about the ways you're trying to control situations, it's time to redirect your energy and apply the Spiritually Aligned Action Method. Choose one area of your life that you've been controlling, and begin to apply the method to it over the next week.

1. **Tap into the inspiration behind your desire, and see how that inspiration serves the world.** In your journal make a list of all the ways that your desire lights you up and how your light brings service to others. Remember that there is service in your joy as long as it doesn't come at another's expense. Your desire for joy is not selfish. Your joy is a gift to the world and to everyone around you.

2. **Believe the Universe will deliver.** In your journal, write clearly what you desire, and then surrender it by adding, "This or something better." Then spend time every day in silent meditation in order to align your energy with the service and inspiration behind your desire. In your meditation, let go of all doubts and questions, and let yourself dream about your vision. Feel into the feelings of inspiration and service behind your desire. Hold visions of yourself fulfilling your desire and all the positive energy you bring to the world. See the people who are elevated in the presence of your desire and joy. Let belief set in. Meditating on the service and inspiration behind your desire helps you believe you are worthy of bringing it to life. For audio guidance in this meditative process, download my free vision-making meditation on the book resources page at GabbyBernstein.com/ SuperAttractor.

3. **Take action from a place of spiritual alignment.** As soon as you feel Steps 1 and 2 take effect, you'll know you're ready to take spiritually aligned action because you'll feel relaxed, faithful, and confident. A sure sign it's time to take action is when you're no longer attached to the outcome. Detachment implies faith. Feel the faith behind your desire, and confidently make your first move. Maybe you pick up the phone, call the woman you've been admiring, and ask her on a date. Or

maybe you propose a bold new project at work. As soon as you feel aligned, take action.

4. **Be patient.** Patience implies you know that what you desire is on the way. When you're patient, you let the Universe do for you what you cannot do for yourself. You clear space for the energy of the Universe to support you in ways you cannot imagine. Practice patience and allow.

To practice patience, use this prayer to let go and allow:

> I lean into the inspiration of my desires, and I know it's enough to lead me toward what is of the highest good. I surrender this desire to the Universe, and I know I'm being guided.

Your patience will be valuable when you're waiting on others to support your desires. Patience creates space for the Universe to work through people. When you're no longer energetically strangling others to make things happen on your schedule, you can set them free to receive their own guidance from the Universe. When someone feels pressured, they can't receive the messages they need in order to support your desires. This is an important lesson I've learned to apply with my team. As an entrepreneur, I've had to practice a lot of patience. As soon as I let go, apply the Spiritually Aligned Action Method, and embrace patience, my team shows up in the most magnificent ways. They present me with ideas that I never could have thought of, and they make creative decisions without relying on me to call the shots. Let other people off the hook so that they can allow the Universe to move through them.

Patient people give off an energy of expansion, peace, and grace. That vibrational frequency is exactly what the Universe responds to. Watch with patience as the amazing gifts of your creation naturally come into form. Admire the work and the timing of the Universe. If you let go and allow, you'll be in awe of what transpires.

PAY ATTENTION TO HOW IT FEELS TO TAKE SPIRITUALLY ALIGNED ACTION

After a week of practicing the Spiritually Aligned Action Method, document your experience in your Super Attractor journal. Describe in great detail exactly how it feels to take action from this state. Maybe you feel free and easygoing. Maybe you breathe easily, no longer obsessed with an outcome. Write it down so you can remember the feeling and your emotional state. Acknowledging how you feel when you take spiritually aligned action will help you the next time you take an action. Become crystal clear about the difference between how it feels to take action from fear versus faith. Know this difference intimately so that you can catch yourself in the moment and pivot. When you notice yourself misaligned with your actions, return to the four-step method and realign. Taking action from any space other than spiritual alignment won't support your desires.

THE PROMISES OF THE SPIRITUALLY ALIGNED ACTION METHOD

When you practice this method consistently, you'll no longer feel the need to control your life. You'll feel empowered by the actions that you take. In many ways you'll feel like a new person. When you stop controlling and start allowing, you begin to notice your nervous system shift. This happened for me in the most incredible way! When I truly surrendered to the Spiritually Aligned Action Method and made it my default, my life totally transformed. I was less stressed, my mind was clear, and my body was relaxed. I felt more supported by the Universe and other people, and

I sensed divine guidance every step of the way. Best of all, I felt serene knowing that my spiritually aligned actions were enough to set my desires in motion. I knew I'd done my part and that the more patient I became, the more I'd receive. I learned how to get out of the way and stop interfering with the natural order.

My hope is that this method will empower you, support you, and most importantly give you peace. When you start to trust that your aligned actions are enough, you can stop pushing and start receiving. This is an amazing way to live! If you're someone who's been trying to control life, I strongly encourage you to make this method your highest priority. Even if you don't apply any of the other principles in the book and just master this one method, you'll feel your Super Attractor power increase immensely. I want to hear your miracles! Diligently practice this method for one month, and then I welcome you to email me through the resources page at GabbyBernstein.com/SuperAttractor and let me know what happens. I want to celebrate your miracles with you!

Applying the Spiritually Aligned Action Method is a great service to the world. When you take action from a place of inspiration, service, and faith, the Universe can create momentum that will have a big impact on others. The story I manifested on the front page of the Sunday Styles section was not just an awesome manifestation—it was a divine service to the world. That story put my spiritual teachings in front of new seekers, aiding them in the discovery of their own spiritual paths.

A week after the story came out, I received a call from a young woman named Nicole, who lived in New York City. When I got on the phone with her, she said, "I read this article in the Sunday Styles section, and it's exactly what I needed! I've been struggling to find purpose and happiness, and your work inspired me to shift my focus and open to a spiritual path." That conversation led Nicole to begin coaching privately with me. We worked together for a few years, and her life changed dramatically. She began to welcome a world beyond the fast-paced New York life, the fashion magazine she worked at, or her social status. She embraced a spiritual life that gave her everything she desired. Today, more than a decade later, Nicole is a trusted authority on wellness, a spiritual guide to her community, and a deeply aligned mother. She and I are dear friends, and I'm so proud of her contribution to the world. Nicole and I both know that the story she read over brunch about a young woman on a spiritual path was the catalyst for her own awakening, which redirected the course of her life.

When you take spiritually aligned action, your desires will be supported in ways you couldn't ever have imagined. You can trust that following this method will speed up your attracting, give you a great sense of tranquility, and support the world! Your service-backed desire, faith, and patience put you into energetic alignment with the Universe, clearing the way for miracles far beyond anything you could "make" happen.

Practicing the Spiritually Aligned Action Method sets you up to claim your desires when the Universe delivers them. A powerful way we claim our desires and multiply miracles is by appreciating and appreciating more! In the next chapter, I guide you to make appreciation a daily practice. When you freely, openly, and constantly appreciate everything that is thriving, every valuable lesson you've learned, and every miracle you receive, you become a magnet for greatness. Turn the page, and welcome the power of appreciation.

Chapter 9

APPRECIATE AND APPRECIATE MORE

In 2012, as part of my book tour for *Spirit Junkie*, my U.K. publishers, Hay House, invited me to London. I'd never been there before, so it was especially nice to be greeted by Hay House's young, enthusiastic publicist Jessica. She was close to my age and a real go-getter. Jessica was so excited to welcome me. She had my two weeks organized and planned perfectly. Not only had she coordinated several events, but she'd also landed me some of the best media placements in the country. I was blown away by her hard work, professionalism, and engaging personality. And to top it off, she introduced me to her favorite spots for high tea and fancy cakes!

Jessica and I spent a lot of time together in those two weeks. I really relied on her, and there was something about her energy that made me feel very taken care of. Toward the end of the tour, we took a trip to Birmingham, where I was scheduled to give a talk. It was a real adventure! We met at the train station and set out north on the two-and-a-half-hour journey. On that train ride, we started talking about everything that we were hoping to manifest in our lives. I confided in Jessica and said, "I'm meeting my boyfriend in

Paris next week, and I think he's going to propose to me." She responded, "That's such a coincidence, because I'm traveling with my boyfriend to Portugal in two weeks, and I have a sense he'll propose too!"

We excitedly talked about how we saw our futures with our soon-to-be fiancés, the children we hoped to have, and our careers. The one thing we both wanted most in our lives was the freedom to do what brought us joy. Jessica opened up to me and said that even though she loved living in London and was so grateful for her job, one day she hoped to live in a slower-paced, more peaceful country town. She dreamed of having a job that would let her work from home with her children. I listened to her closely and said, "With your skills you could work from anywhere. People are always looking for great publicists and planners!" I went on and on about how much I appreciated her expertise and hard work. I complimented her work ethic and expressed my deep appreciation. Then out of nowhere I said, "Maybe one day we'll work together. Imagine that?!"

She said, "That would be a dream!"

After my successful U.K. trip, I headed to Paris, filled with appreciation for Jessica and all her support. As I expected, Zach proposed to me in Paris! I was elated. Upon returning to New York, I emailed Jessica to tell her the news. She responded that her boyfriend had proposed as well! The desires we had talked about on the train had started manifesting.

Four years went by, and I continued to work with Jessica whenever I visited the U.K. Each year we became closer friends. In that time, her position at Hay House U.K. rose to the level of events director. I witnessed Jessica really own her confidence in the work—she was thriving. Despite all her success, I wasn't surprised to get an email from her to say that she was moving to the countryside and looking for a new job outside the city. She was sad to leave her big job at Hay House but knew it was the right decision for her future. She wanted to have a child, work from home, and live with the ease that a long commute to London wouldn't allow for.

In many respects, Jessica and I were tracking at the same pace. Zach and I had started to spend most of our time outside of New York City. At this time I was consciously slowing down and repeating my life mantra, "Everything is happening around me, and I'm truly taken care of." I was manifesting more support in my career, and I was open to creative possibilities. The day I received the email from Jessica that she'd left Hay House and moved to the country, a loud inner voice spoke through me and said, "Work with her!" I had no idea how this would make sense since I wasn't looking to hire an event planner or a publicist. But I knew how hard she worked and how smart she was, and I had a sense that she'd be able to figure out whatever I threw her way. So I followed my gut and called Jessica immediately to offer her a position. She accepted on the spot. Within one month of working with Jessica, it was clear that she was going to be an integral part of my team.

Now Jessica is living in the country with her husband and their baby, working with me as a senior project manager! She reminds me regularly how grateful she is to work with such a mission-driven company, help a lot of people, and have a lot of fun. We have given each other freedom, security, and growth. A little dream and a lot of appreciation brought our desires into form. Not a day goes by when I don't appreciate Jessica for all that she brings to my business and my life. Our mutual appreciation has created a working relationship beyond our wildest dreams. We got everything we hoped for!

I believe that this divine manifestation came out of the energy of appreciation. The feelings of appreciation and enthusiasm we felt on that train in 2012 sent out a clear desire to the Universe. Our appreciation for each other released all resistance and doubt. Appreciation cleared the path for the manifestation to happen naturally and at the perfect time.

One of the most important elements of co-creating the life you desire is to let appreciation lead you. Whatever you appreciate you create more of. This is because when you're in a state of appreciation, you're in vibrational alignment with your true love nature. Appreciation is an energy of acceptance and nonresistance—and without resistance we are Super Attractors. In a state of appreciation, you're relaxed, surrendered, and faithful. That is the perfect energy for allowing your desires to come into form. When you're aligned with appreciation, you can surrender your desires to the Universe and trust in a plan beyond your own. That was the case for Jessica and me. We focused on appreciation, and the Universe led us in the right direction.

APPRECIATION GETS YOU OUT OF YOUR OWN WAY

The goal of this book is to help you release control and allow the Universe to support your desires. The fastest way to let go of control is to be in a state of appreciation. When you assume this energy, you feel good in the present moment regardless of whether your desires have manifested, and you're having fun along the way to what you want. When we're in a state of appreciation, we're actively allowing more of what we want to come toward us while dissolving the blocks to the presence of our Super Attractor power.

APPRECIATION CONNECTS YOU TO YOUR SUPER ATTRACTOR POWER

When your focus is on what's working and thriving, you feel good, and that good-feeling state is what attracts more of what you want. But many people act in ways that are completely contrary to this. They obsess over what's not working because they feel hopeless. Or they frequently complain, which may offer some temporary relief from their discomfort but nothing more. Fixating on the negative only creates more of what we don't want, whereas focusing on what we can appreciate in our lives moves us to a better point of attraction. Almost all of us can be thankful and grateful for some aspect of our world.

Often when I share this suggestion with people, it's met with some resistance. People say things like "But if I appreciate this bad situation, I'll stay stuck here." They think their appreciation tells the Universe that they're happy right where they are.

In fact, their appreciation is their ticket out. Focusing on feeling good is much more valuable than focusing on your exact desire or goal. The Universe responds to *energy* and delivers circumstances and opportunities that are a vibrational match. If your desire feels far from reach, concentrate on what feels good and you'll get closer to your desire. Let the Universe respond swiftly to your good-feeling emotions, and before you know it, you'll be closer to what you really want.

Appreciating what you do have puts you in the right state of mind to receive better opportunities, and it makes you more receptive to creative solutions you otherwise might have missed. It clears space for you to pay attention to the kindness and support of others. There is powerful energy behind the emotion of appreciation, and it will elevate you, open your mind, and make you a magnet for what you desire.

You don't have to find appreciation for the things that aren't working. Instead, appreciate anything else—whatever isn't working will benefit. Assuming an energy of appreciation is the fastest way out of a negative obsession. A great example is my friend Alex. He made a bad business decision that he couldn't get out of. For months he obsessed about what he could've done differently and how much better things could be if he hadn't made this choice. His point of attraction was focused on what wasn't working rather than what was. And the more he tried to get out of the negativity, the more negative he felt. This is because sometimes when we try really hard to move out of a negative stance, we actually bring more energy to it. Finally Alex hit bottom with his negative obsession and came to me for help. In an effort to guide him to a new energy, I asked him what he appreciated in his life right now. His first response was, "A lot, actually, but it feels far from reach because all I can think about is this big mistake." I explained to him that in this moment he wasn't going to be able to think his way out of his negative story, but he could shift his focus. Willing to play along, Alex started reaching for appreciation. He talked about how he appreciated his wife and kids. He appreciated our friendship. He appreciated his ability to learn from his mistakes. And then he blurted out, "Wow, I actually appreciate this mistake because now I won't make it again!" In a matter of seconds Alex was able to think his way out of his negative story through appreciation. His general appreciation gently led him to even appreciate his given circumstances.

Try this out! Take an area of your life where you wish things were different. Maybe you want a fulfilling romantic relationship. Instead of focusing on how hard it is to date and how much you can't stand the people you're set up with, reach for something that you appreciate about your life right now. Think about the fulfilling relationship you have with a close friend. Appreciate your family and your community. By appreciating the relationships that are working, you change your energy about relationships overall. You can also go more general with your thoughts, appreciating your health, your creative projects, or anything else that makes you feel great. Maybe you want to manifest more abundance into your life, but all you think about is your debt. Start appreciating the abundance you do have. Appreciate your access to this book. Appreciate the internet as a powerful resource for finding new employment or making money online. As soon as you redirect your focus, you'll embody the feeling of abundance necessary to be a Super Attractor. That feeling is what will attract more abundance into your life.

MAKE APPRECIATION A HABIT

There are many ways to make appreciation a habit. A great way is to begin your day with it! Write three to five pages of appreciation in your journal every morning. Abraham-Hicks refer to this exercise as "a rampage of appreciation." As you fill each page with what you appreciate, the love within you will expand, and you'll feel awesome. You can write about the simplest things. Write about how you appreciate your comfortable bed, your morning coffee, the work you do, the friends you have. Or as my dear friend Joe Watson would say, "Be thankful for getting up in the morning, everything else is gravy." You can get really specific and write about how you appreciate yourself for the way you handled a situation the day before. Just get into a fast flow of appreciation and let your pen glide across the pages. You can also do this journaling exercise before you go to sleep. If you fall asleep in a state of appreciation, you raise your vibration while you rest. When you wake up in the morning, you'll feel no resistance, only love.

APPRECIATE AND APPRECIATE MORE

Once you start to cultivate a feeling of appreciation, continue to reach for more. When you get into the flow of appreciation, you want to create even more momentum behind it. As soon as you start to smile, feel good, and possibly even get tingly or teary-eyed from your appreciation, keep going! Reach for more reasons to be appreciative. As you guide your thoughts toward more and more appreciation, you build momentum and magnify your good-feeling vibration.

Our fearful egos will often try to stifle our positive momentum. The ego's inner dialogue of fear is perpetuated by negative thoughts and beliefs. We've grown to rely on those fear-based beliefs to maintain a false sense of control and safety. But our true safety lies in our capacity to align with the love of the Universe. That's why it's so important to proactively notice your good feelings and reach for more of them. Appreciate and appreciate more. Let the feelings flow freely so that you can feel a swell of energy in your body. When you feel appreciation set in, you can start to think about more things that you appreciate. Ride the wave of good-feeling emotions to take advantage of your positive flow. Notice what happens when you reach for more. You may feel more energized. People around you will be lit up in your presence. Inspired ideas will surface naturally, and you'll feel strongly connected to a higher power. When you let appreciation flow through you, you become one with the love of the Universe.

You may even want to share your appreciation with someone else, as they will benefit big-time from your high vibes. If you're feeling gratitude for someone in your life, go out of your way to tell them. Appreciation is contagious and has the power to totally shift the energy of a relationship. My husband and I have a practice of sharing our appreciation for each other the moment we wake up. The first words out of our mouths are, "I appreciate you because _____." We list several reasons why we love and appreciate one another. Those mornings when we rush out of bed and skip our appreciation never have the same flow and positive energy as the days that begin with this practice. Make appreciation a habit so that you can effortlessly maintain a state of positive flow in your life.

APPRECIATE YOUR MANIFESTATIONS

Don't forget to express your appreciation once your desires manifest in your life! There's a really common phenomenon that occurs when people's manifestations come into form. At first they're excited . . . but soon the inner voice of fear pipes up to sabotage the party. The voice of fear will make you believe that your manifestation is too good to be true or that something could go wrong. This is especially common when you've been waiting a long time to manifest the desire. That's where appreciation comes in. The moment you manifest your desire, go big with appreciation. Sit for a minute or two and reflect on how grateful you are for what you've created. Don't push past the moment of manifestation. Celebrate it!

Your manifestation may ignite fear when you attract something that you struggle to keep. For example, a friend of mine has no trouble manifesting relationships but struggles to keep them. It's the same story over and over: the relationship starts off great, but within six months the guy drops off the radar. Each time her relationship ends, it's as if she's replaying a scene in a mini drama. By the time she came to me for advice, she was blaming herself for the loss of these relationships. She kept saying, "I must not be interesting enough or smart enough. Is there something wrong with me?" I responded with a lot of compassion and explained that there was absolutely nothing wrong with her. What had gone wrong was her point of focus. She'd never truly let herself get excited about the relationship for fear that she'd lose it. The devastation from the first breakup lingered in the back of her mind during every relationship that followed. Her fear of the relationship ending was the exact reason each new relationship would end. Every time a guy would break up with her, he'd say the same thing: "You're amazing, but something just feels off." What felt off was her resistance and fear.

Does this situation sound familiar? Energetic sabotage can show up in any type of manifestation when we still have lingering resistance. Right when you manifest exactly what you want, the voice of fear will try to take you down. So as soon as you manifest your desires, ward off the ego backlash by going into a deep state of appreciation. The best way to keep your manifestation flourishing is to appreciate it. Let yourself go on an inner journey of appreciation. Think about how proud you are of yourself for attracting this desire. Celebrate the wonderful news, and get excited to experience this new way of being. Bring only positivity and appreciation to your sacred manifestations. This practice will not only help you enjoy what you've manifested, but it will also elevate your energy so that you continue to manifest even more. Good things come to those who feel good.

APPRECIATION IS THE ANTIDOTE TO WORRY

I'm a recovering worrier. I've spent countless hours worrying about things I couldn't control. Thankfully, over time I've built up a strong spiritual practice and accumulated many tools to help me find my way out of the chaos of worry.

The best tool of all has been appreciation. When you're in a state of appreciation, there's no room for worry, because they cannot coexist. Whenever I notice myself worrying about something out of my control, I immediately start listing reasons to feel appreciative. These appreciations can be related to the issue I'm worrying about or not—it doesn't matter. What matters is that I'm shifting my focus off the addictive pattern of worrying and onto the positive habit of appreciation. The moment I redirect my focus, the worry dissolves. Some days I put this practice to use multiple times. I've done it so often now that appreciation is my default mode!

We spend a lot of time focusing on what we're experiencing rather than how we're experiencing it. We forget that we can change our experience of anything simply by shifting our point of focus. Any situation can be experienced with more love when we choose to see it through the lens of appreciation. Even the tough times can be seen through this lens. When you choose a perspective of appreciation, you can find great growth opportunities instead of remaining the victim of your experience. For example, when I think back about hitting bottom with my drug and alcohol addiction in 2005, I have nothing but appreciation. My deep gratitude for my recovery is what has kept me clean and sober for so many years. I appreciate my addiction because it was the catalyst for the spiritual path that I am on today. I don't judge myself for being a recovering alcoholic and addict. I celebrate it! Through appreciation I've been able to turn what could have been a shameful time in my life into a miracle. I look back on my rock bottom and thank the Universe for all the divine lessons and clear direction on my path. Most importantly, I appreciate my addiction because through my recovery I've been able to help others get sober too.

When you choose to perceive your experiences through the lens of appreciation, you can reframe something very uncomfortable into a miracle. You can choose to appreciate a heartbreak as an opportunity to deeply feel, or you can appreciate a diagnosis as the catalyst for putting you on a healing path. Appreciation gives you a perspective that is aligned with the love of the Universe. When you see your life through this lens, you can assume the energy of acceptance. By finding things to appreciate, you can easily accept even a difficult experience as a great learning device on your spiritual journey. Let appreciation clear your path and guide you forward.

APPRECIATE THE PEOPLE IN YOUR LIFE, EVEN THOSE WHO TRIGGER YOU

When you begin to devote your attention to what you appreciate about others, you immediately feel relief. In my book *Judgment Detox*, there's a chapter called "See for the First Time." In that chapter I suggest that readers focus their practice on someone they've been resenting, and I ask them to list everything they appreciate about that person. The purpose is to consciously choose to see that person in their light—to accept our oneness and see that the love within them is a reflection of our own.

This step can be challenging for people who feel that they've been treated badly. In these cases, I suggest that they appreciate what they were able to learn from the relationship, even if it was painful. I tell them that I applied this practice to current and past relationships in my own life and experienced miraculous results. By practicing seeing for the first time and appreciating people whom I'd been resenting, I began to feel a newfound freedom. I felt released from attack thoughts as forgiveness set in, and I was able to liberate myself from daily feelings of anger.

Appreciating the people who have hurt us helps us release the energetic hold they have on us. When we resent others, we block our Super Attractor power because our resentment keeps us in a low vibrational state. Forgiveness is necessary if we're going to live with ease and effortlessly attract more of what we want. Let appreciation be your guide to releasing the attachments you have to your attack thoughts and past resentments. When you release the past, you clear space to attract what you want in the present.

Meditate on appreciation

A powerful way to connect to being a Super Attractor is to meditate on the feeling of appreciation. Within minutes of your meditation practice, you can become like a magnet for what you want! Follow these steps to bring yourself into alignment with the Universe and tune in to your power. (Go to GabbyBernstein.com/SuperAttractor to download the guided audio version of this meditation.)

- Prepare to meditate by finding a silent space and getting comfortable. Open your journal and write out one full page of appreciation.

- Press play on an uplifting song you love. Be sure to choose a song that makes you feel really good.

- Sit in meditation while listening to the song, and think about all the things you appreciate. Let your mind wander into more and more appreciation. Allow positive emotions to flow through you. Feel the feelings and let them flow.

- Ride the momentum of the good feelings.

- When you're ready, gently come out of your meditation and pick up your journal. Once again let your pen flow, and continue to write about what you appreciate. Write until you feel complete.

This appreciation meditation practice will feel great. When you attune your energy to these good-feeling emotions, you will instantly notice a major shift. You'll feel more alive and awake. Inspiration will pour through you, people will want to spend more time with you, and your attracting will speed up. There are countless times in my life when I've witnessed amazing Universal support and wild synchronicity after practicing an appreciation meditation. Follow this practice, and witness how quickly your manifesting will speed up. Most importantly, celebrate how great you feel!

When you appreciate others and yourself, it's the closest you can get to becoming a match with the energy of the Universe. When our energy matches the energy of love, that is when we are truly Super Attractors. From this energetic state, anything is possible. You can heal the past, attract what you want in the present, and know that the future will unfold in whatever way is of the highest good. In this state of love, you are powerful beyond measure because you're aligned with the source of who you are. There is no resistance in this state. There's only love. That love is what dissolves all boundaries and clears the path. We think we need to try hard to get what we want when all we really have to do is stop trying and start appreciating. Appreciation has the power to put you into a relaxed state in which you are receptive to the positive flow of the Universe. In this state of receptivity, your Super Attractor power is at an all-time high, and you're primed to manifest your desires. Stop trying and start appreciating.

Appreciation will play a big role in the coming chapter. In Chapter 10 you will be guided to strengthen your faith in the Universe. The more appreciation you embody, the easier it will be to rely on the power of the Universe and believe you're worthy of miracles. Carry your appreciation into the next chapter, and faith will surely set in.

One moment of appreciation at a time has guided my greatest manifestations. Today, six years after that train ride in London, Jessica and I still embody the energy of appreciation. We appreciate our friendship, our business collaboration, and the great work we can do in this world. We appreciate the incredible team of people we have the privilege of working with. And we appreciate you, our reader, for giving us the best reason to wake up and get to work each day. Our friendship and business relationship is God's creation because it was born out of appreciation. And it's that same appreciation that continues to propel us forward as we create a movement throughout the world. As I close this chapter, I think about my morning appreciation journal, and I celebrate that Jessica is always at the top of the page.

May appreciation clear your path as it has mine. I know that the moment you begin applying the practices in this chapter, you will experience miracles. Focus your attention on that good-feeling emotion, and notice your positive feelings increase. Now that you're feeling better, appreciate your ability to shift your energy so quickly. Look for even more things to appreciate, and continue to celebrate how great it feels. Trust in this process, and know that the more you attune to the energy of appreciation, the more the Universe will deliver.

Chapter 10

LET THE UNIVERSE CATCH UP WITH YOUR DREAMS

In March of 2017, I was working hard to heal core wounds from my past, releasing control of my business, and learning how to trust people to support me. I was also in my third year of trying to conceive. I had a deep desire to be a mother, but I continued to run into emotional roadblocks. It seemed that the Universe wanted me to focus on my own healing. While my Higher Self could see that there was big spiritual work for me to do, my logical side was frustrated and sad. Still, I diligently tracked my ovulation and tried my hardest to make it happen. But the more I tried to control my conception, the more disappointed I became. Why was I a Super Attractor in every other area of my life, but couldn't attract my baby?

One afternoon I sat in my office, gazing out the window in a state of desperation. I felt defeated and sad and ashamed. I'd been writing and speaking publicly about my desire to conceive. In doing so, I was trying hard to be a beacon of hope for my readers and audience members, but in that moment my own hope was far from reach. It was difficult for me to harness my faith and feel my connection to the Universe. I needed a spiritual intervention.

I closed my eyes, sat in stillness, and took a deep breath. I said a prayer to the Universe: "Once again, I surrender this desire, and I welcome guidance." When I opened my eyes, something appeared in my peripheral vision. Two huge wild turkeys were walking slowly across my lawn. These turkeys redirected my attention from discouragement to contentment. My emotions traveled right up the emotional scale the second I shifted my focus off myself and onto these beautiful animals. I watched them walk down the slope of the lawn, pecking at patches of grass along the way. I was in awe of their peace and tranquility as the late-winter snow fell on their backs. It was a real meditative moment and a beautiful shift in perception that helped me to move from despair to hope and realign with the Universe.

Later that afternoon I invited my husband to meditate with me. From time to time, I sit with him and invite our guides to speak through me and give us direction. I often find that I can connect to my guides best when I'm speaking, so when I meditate with Zach and invite my guides to speak through me, great wisdom can be revealed. The guides also love to visit us together. We sat in meditation, and I invited my spirit guides of the highest truth and compassion to enter our meditation and give us clear direction. Within moments I began to feel my hands tingle and a warm energy of love pass over my body. We sat in silence for a few minutes, and then my guides began to direct my thoughts. Words that were not mine started to come through. The guides assured us that the Universe had a plan for our child. They encouraged us to be patient and to trust in the timing of the Universe. Then they suggested I Google the spiritual meaning of wild turkeys. I laughed out loud and explained to Zach about my earlier moment with the turkeys on the lawn. Clearly the turkeys had come to bring me a message.

When we came out of our meditation, we went to my computer and Googled "spiritual meaning behind wild turkeys." I clicked on the first search result, and at the top of the page, it said, "The spiritual meaning of wild turkeys is fertility." Zach and I gasped at the powerful message we'd received. I began to cry with gratitude for the spiritual wisdom that was available to me all the time.

That day was another turning point in my fertility journey. I saw it as a new opportunity to surrender more and deepen my faith in a plan beyond my own. Once again I accepted that surrender and faith in the Universe were required in order for me to truly co-create my desires. Even though my desire hadn't manifested, this experience helped me stay faithful. That day I made the commitment to release time and let the Universe show me what to do.

When we truly surrender our desires to the Universe, a mighty force of faith can set in. That faith offers us clear direction when we're lost. When we assume an energy of faith, we are receptive, released, and magnetic. The energy of faith is an energy of allowing. When we allow the guidance of the Universe to direct us, we can take our hands off the steering wheel and be led. My faith gave me a sense of certainty and freedom. I knew that I could stop controlling and start allowing. The energy of allowing felt so much better to me. It felt natural and empowering.

In the following months, whenever I'd start to lose hope, I'd turn to the image of the turkeys in the snow. I held on to my guides' divine message, and I continued to return to faith. The miracle wasn't that I was pregnant just yet but that I was faithful my child was on the way. Faith is the greatest miracle of all because when we're faithful, we feel good, and when we feel good, the Universe will conspire to bring forth our desires.

At the end of 2017, I was preparing for a book launch. I felt overwhelmed by the work and travel ahead of me. In moments of stress, I could lose track of my faith and lean into doubt. I was driving on a country road, and my mind began to wander to all my to-do lists, goals, and expectations. In that stressed state, I thought, "When will my baby be able to come? How can I conceive when I have this much going on?" As I started to become more frantic, I suddenly noticed that a new song was playing on my car stereo. The song was "Bow to You," by Jaya Lakshmi and Ananda. The lyrics were so profound that they redirected my focus off my fear and uncertainty and onto the energy of love.

I listened as they sang, "You're the Creator. You're the Sustainer. You're the Destroyer of all. You're my lover. You're my partner. You're my teacher of all. And I bow to you. And I bow to you. And I bow to you. And I bow to you." The lyrics moved me so deeply that I began to cry. They locked me into the energy of the Universe and the presence of a God of my own understanding. I started chanting out loud to the song: "I bow to you. I bow to you." The tears flowed down my face as I sensed the presence of a child in the car with me. I felt as if there were a baby sitting behind me in the backseat. And I heard that child say, "I'm coming in March. Be patient and trust." I felt this presence so strongly that I could not deny it. I continued to chant, "I bow to you. I bow to you." Once again, I'd received the spiritual guidance that I needed to sustain my faith.

Each time I surrendered, I was guided to surrender more. My willingness to let the Universe lead helped me stay on track and maintain strong faith amid uncertainty and feelings of lack.

February rolled around, and with my latest book launch behind me, I started to do the pregnancy math. I figured that if I conceived in February, I'd get the news of my child in early March, keeping in line with the message I had received in my car several months ago. I started getting hopeful that maybe the message would come true. Once again, I had a plan of my own.

March came, and I had high expectations of a positive pregnancy test.

Instead, I got my period. I fell back into that well-worn place of defeat. I was frustrated with the Universe. Why wasn't my guidance showing up for me the way I'd heard it? But despite my disappointment and sadness, I knew once again that the answer was to turn inward. Even though I was questioning my faith, the voice of my Higher Self was louder than the voice of fear. I knew that if I sat in my meditation, I could realign with my truth and receive more guidance to keep me on my path. So I returned to the guidance of love. I had committed to respond to fear with faith and to call on spiritual support. I sat in meditation and asked for another sign. This time I asked for a specific sign that had great meaning to me on my fertility journey. I knew that Archangel Gabriel, the angel who helped with maternity and fertility, was guiding me. And I knew that he was often depicted holding lilies. So I asked Gabriel to show me a lily to once again restore my faith and guide my path.

The next day I walked into my husband's office still feeling down. I sat on Zach's lap and placed my phone on his desk. Zach embraced me and said, "Everything is working out in the perfect time." The second he said those words, a song began to play on my phone. This was odd, considering my phone had been locked when I placed it on his desk. I went to turn it off but was shocked when I saw the album name on the screen. The album was called *I See the Sign*, and the song was called "Way Go Lily." I sat back on my husband's lap and said, "This is our sign! Let's listen." I took the sign as another reminder from the Universe that my faith is stronger than my fear. We sat back and received the most incredible guidance. The artist, Sam Amidon, sang the word *lily* over and over. The Universe spoke directly to us once again. Just as I had with the turkeys and the song in my car, I continued to feel guided. This was one of the loudest and clearest signs I'd ever received: The album *I See the Sign* played the song "Way Go Lily" when my phone was completely locked. Not to mention I'd never heard this song before and didn't have it saved on any playlist. I burst into tears of joy. It felt so wonderful to receive this clear guidance.

When we lose faith, we have two choices: We can get hooked into our fear story and try to control our desires. Or we can surrender to the Universe and welcome guidance to restore our faith. Whenever you choose the latter, you will be guided back to faith and love. Faith is always available to you when you suspend your disbelief and let the Universe and spirit guide you back to your right mind of love. Faith in the Universe is easy to access when you're willing to receive. No matter how often you detour into fear, you can always call on Universal guidance to lead you back to faith in love.

Spirit guided me back to love on that March day when "Way Go Lily" began playing. Today, as I write this chapter, I'm listening to the song "Way Go Lily" in the background, feeling in awe of the guidance that I received. Today is July 28, exactly 120 days from March 30, the day I conceived my baby boy. This day is significant because in the yogic tradition, the 120th day after conception is the day that the soul enters the mother's body and chooses to be in this world. As the Universe would have it, my child showed up right on time. At the end of March, our baby boy was conceived.

When I woke up this morning, I knew it was time to write this chapter. I knew it was time for my spirit guides and me to celebrate my incredible journey of conception and my willingness to be guided. Conceiving my child is one of the greatest miracles I've ever received. What makes it so miraculous is the opportunity I have had to practice surrender and strengthen my faith. The true miracle is having faith no matter what. If your desires haven't come into form yet, please know that each time you return to faith, you're receiving the ultimate gift from the Universe. Living with faith will help you feel whole, safe, and supported even when you don't have everything you want or think you need. Faith in a higher power is the greatest gift you can ask for.

My faith also gave me patience to trust that the Universe has a better plan than mine. I celebrate the Universal timing above my own. My child was conceived at a time when I felt safe, healthy, and secure. I celebrate my body for healing enough to carry a child. I celebrate my husband for being my faith when I got off track. I celebrate my willingness to surrender my desires for three years as I allowed the Universe to catch up with my dreams. As I write this chapter, I'm halfway through my pregnancy, and I already see my child as my greatest teacher. He has already given me the gift of surrender, and he helped me deepen my faith in the Universe. Dear child, I bow to you . . .

THE PATHWAY TO FAITH

Profound guidance can be revealed when we become willing to let the Universe catch up with our dreams.

Synchronicity, support, and clear direction are available to you right now if you're ready to surrender. If you've lost sight of your faith, let this story remind you that there is a plan and a timeline beyond your own. See this as an opportunity to surrender more and strengthen your faith by allowing the wisdom of the Universe to move through you.

It is my intention to align you with faith that you are a Super Attractor. With this faith you can be led by the Universe. I want you to know the experience of receiving spiritual guidance. When you allow this guidance into your life, you'll trust every step of the plan that unfolds.

Follow the method I've outlined below, and let the Universe catch up with your dreams.

TURN OVER YOUR PLANS

Becoming faithful requires that we surrender our plans, our timeline, and our agenda so that we can allow the Universe to guide us. As you know by now, our plans and our desire to control can get in the way of the guidance we long for most. We carry a false belief that we know what's best and that we can make it happen, whatever "it" is. For example, during my conception journey, I spent several years trying to control the timeline and outcome—eating certain foods, timing my ovulation, and future tripping about the whole thing. Pouring all my energy into planning and controlling gave me no space for faith. But when I finally turned my plans over the Universe, I was given clear direction. Surrendering my plans to a higher power gave me freedom to slow down, listen, and receive. In that receptive state, I could hear my inner wisdom and my spirit guides. I was gifted certainty, signs, and strong faith. I stopped playing God and let God work through healers, doctors, friends, my husband, and my own body. I could let go and allow.

The pathway to faith always starts with surrender. But let's get honest—surrendering your desires to the Universe can seem difficult and feel scary. Our fearful ego has convinced us that surrendering means giving up on our desires, our control, and our ability to take action. The truth is that surrender is the first step to receiving. If turning over your desires and offering up your plans feels uncomfortable, don't worry. If you want to feel free in this moment, that's enough to begin this process.

Take a moment to read this prayer:

Thank you, Universe and guides of the highest truth and compassion. I am ready to feel free. I welcome a newfound faith.

Now say the prayer out loud, and take a moment to settle into the feelings of what it means to surrender to faith in the Universe.

Take notice of how you feel. Do you sense resistance to turning over your plans? Do you not trust that the Universe can handle all that you need and want? Honor your resistance, but continue to practice choosing again. When you notice thoughts of resistance, choose again by reciting this prayer. Memorize the prayer, and say it as often as possible. Say it out loud or silently whenever you notice yourself trying to control your desires. Get into a moment-to-moment habit of turning over your desires to the care of a higher power. The more you pray for relief, the more freedom you will feel. Trust in the power of this prayer, and set yourself up for surrender.

Our greatest spiritual shifts don't come through force; they come through freedom. When we pray, we welcome freedom from resistance. Recognize that surrender doesn't require much action at all. All that is required is your desire to feel free and your willingness to ask the Universe for help.

Make this prayer your daily mantra, and call on it regularly to reconnect you with the Super Attractor force within.

ASK FOR CLEAR DIRECTION

Once you've aligned your energy with the Universe through your prayer, you will begin to feel a subtle shift. It may not be totally obvious at first, but the prayer for faith will help you feel a connection to a power greater than you. Each time you say your prayer, you remind yourself of the ever-present energy of love that is supporting you. Once you recall that connection, you are primed to ask for direction. It's at this point that you can ask the Universe for clarity, signs, symbols, and guidance. Receiving signs from the Universe is like a spiritual pat on the back and a gentle reminder that you are indeed on the right path.

In my book *The Universe Has Your Back*, I introduced the practice of asking the Universe for a sign. My sign was an owl. Whenever I felt resistance and control get in the way of my Super Attractor connection, I'd surrender my plans and ask the Universe to show me an owl to help guide my path. Some days I'd ask the Universe to help me make a specific decision and show me an owl if my choice was in the right direction. Other days I'd simply ask the Universe to show me an owl to remind me that I was being guided. People all throughout the world have messaged me about the signs they used and the incredible guidance they received. Readers asked for signs like butterflies, ladybugs, and songs on the radio. The clearer they were about their signs, the easier it was to communicate with the Universe and receive direction.

As you read in my conception story, the Universe offered me many clear signs that directed my path. The signs came in the form of an inner voice, a song playing out of nowhere, images of lilies, and a great sense of connection to the presence of love around me. These signs were so undeniable that I had no other choice but to wholeheartedly believe in the spiritual presence beyond my physical realm. Each time I received a sign, my faith would multiply. I want you to know that sense of faith and certainty in the Universe. I want you to receive your signs, to sense the flow of the Universe, and to feel the angelic presence of support guiding your path.

Receiving this connection can happen fast when you're willing. As I taught in Chapter 7, the only thing that blocks this guidance is your resistance. So I ask you to suspend your disbelief, even temporarily, as you follow this practice. It's time to start asking for signs and paying attention to the guidance you receive.

There are many ways you can ask the Universe for guidance. Choose one of the practices below and commit to it for a week.

ASK THE UNIVERSE FOR A SIGN

Getting into a dialogue with the Universe can be very powerful, especially when you're clear about the guidance you want to receive. The clearer you are about what you're asking for, the clearer the response will be. If you're struggling to make a decision or feeling uncertain about an outcome, ask the Universe for a sign that you're on the right track. Choose the first thing that comes to your mind, and don't second-guess it. You want to be very clear about the sign you're asking for. As I shared in *The Universe Has Your Back*, when I was contemplating a big decision about choosing a house, I asked the Universe to show me an owl to confirm that the home was right for me. If you have read that book, you already know that owls showed up everywhere! My clear signs gave me the direction that I needed to buy the home, which ultimately redirected the course of my life.

Be specific with the Universe about when you'd like to receive your sign. The clearer you are, the easier it will be to receive information. Here's one way that you can ask: "Thank you, Universe, for showing me my sign of ____ within 24 hours if ____ is right for me." Then be patient and let the Universe offer you clear direction. You may be thinking, "What if I don't get my sign?" Well, that's a sign too! Not receiving your sign is guidance that's just as significant. If you asked the Universe to confirm you're in the right romantic relationship, and you don't receive your sign, that's a sign! Take this direction seriously. I'm not saying that you break up with your partner overnight. But I am suggesting that you look more closely at the fundamental issues that need to be resolved. At the end of the day, you will always exercise free will, but consider the signs from the Universe (or lack thereof) as supportive direction on your path.

SPEAK DIRECTLY TO AN ANGEL OR A GUIDE

As you deepen your connection to your spirit guides through the practices in Chapter 7, you will begin to understand the unique ways your guides connect with you. When I was seeking direction around conception, I knew I could ask Archangel Gabriel to show me lilies. If I see a spark of white light, I know it's an angelic presence. When I see a blue light, I know it's Archangel Michael. A green light represents Archangel Raphael and his healing powers, and a golden light represents Archangel Gabriel. Angels and guides will be very clear in their connections and give you ways to differentiate their presence from other guidance. Don't deny the messages you receive from them. Ask your guides and angels to be specific and clear with their communication. Guides will be creative with their delivery of messages. For instance, my friend Aimee's father passed away many years ago. She has always felt him communicate with her through her dreams. In one dream Aimee was visiting me at my house and her father showed up in my living room. He said, "My sign for you is a white SUV. Look out Gabby's window and you'll see one." Aimee woke up confused by this direction, so she called me to help her interpret it. When she shared the dream with me, I gasped and said, "Aimee, I drive a white SUV!" To this day Aimee always knows that her father is guiding her whenever she sees a white SUV. Never question the signs that spirit gives you.

Know that if you're receiving angels' or spirit guides' signs, your energy is receptive, and you're indeed being guided. Get into the practice of asking your guides and angels for a clear sign whenever you need it. Their guidance will reassure you and give you certainty, the same way I felt when I continued to receive my lilies.

SPIRIT SPEAKS THROUGH CHILDREN

As I taught in Chapter 5, when we're young, there's a thin veil between the perceptual world and the spiritual realm. The children in your life are deeply connected to guides, angels, and spiritual support. If you see an infant or toddler smiling and gazing above your head, I like to think they're seeing and connecting with a guide or angel. When they speak to you of their "imaginary friends," don't ignore them! They can see your deceased loved ones, your guides, and angels. Children are often trying to communicate spiritual messages to adults, but far too often they're shut down or ignored.

There are important reasons to nurture your child's spiritual connection. First, they have signs for you! Don't ignore the messages they offer. For instance, my friend Beth has been trying to conceive her second child for two years but has had multiple miscarriages. Her last miscarriage left her deeply depressed. She hadn't spoken to her 3-year-old daughter about losing a child, but her daughter intuitively knew that her mother was distressed. One afternoon her daughter walked over to her and said, "Mama, there is a baby coming to you soon." Beth burst into tears when her daughter said this. She felt a rush of energy move through her as though she was receiving divine spiritual guidance. This was the exact message she needed to hear. Children have great wisdom and guidance for you. Pay attention and be receptive.

Second, nurturing your child's spiritual connection will greatly help them throughout their life. The more you support their spiritual beliefs at a young age, the less likely they will be to lose them. Think about how much easier life might have been if you'd always known that spirit was by your side. If it feels aligned for you, encourage your children to talk to their guides and deepen their connection. It will serve them in great ways.

Stay open and receptive to all of the ways you can receive signs from spirit. It doesn't matter which of these ways you ask for guidance; what matters is that you pay attention to the guidance that you receive. The more signs you receive, the stronger your faith will become. Continue to create spiritual proof through your willingness to ask and receive.

DO NOTHING, AND LET THE UNIVERSE SHOW YOU WHAT TO DO

This next step toward faith is to do nothing and let the Universe show you what to do. One of the greatest ways to enhance your Super Attractor power is to step back and trust you're being guided. All of our doing gets in the way of our receiving. Therefore, get into the practice of not interfering with the Universal guidance that is available to you. If you're not receiving clear direction right away, then be patient, relax, and distract yourself with a fun activity. The sooner you get your ego out of the way, the sooner you will receive guidance. This is the practice of noninterference. When you no longer interfere with the Universal guidance, you can truly fine-tune your receptivity and connection.

Doing nothing is confusing to the ego. When we feel unsettled or uncomfortable with our circumstances, it's natural to want to do something about it. I have a hard time sitting in the discomfort of relationships or issues being unsettled. I like to clear things up fast, work out problems, and live in the solution. But sometimes the solution cannot come from our logic and action. Sometimes we have to be still and listen for the solution to be presented to us by a Universal force beyond our ego's need to feel resolved. The time in between resolutions can feel scary and out of control. But when you do nothing, you clear space to allow loving solutions to be presented.

The next time you're trying to find a solution out of a sense of urgency or fear, take a deep breath. Remember that you have divine guidance available to you, and ask the Universe for help. Then say this prayer: *Thank you, Universal guidance, for guiding me to solutions that are of the highest good for all.* Regardless of whether you say it aloud or not, the Universe is picking up your request for guidance. When you decide not to interfere, your point of focus shifts from trying to fix problems to surrendering to solutions. This is a much more powerful energy to embody. Your new desire is aligned with love, and the Universe will always conspire to bring you what is of the highest good for you and for all. Release your expectations through a prayer, surrender to receive support, and trust that the Universe will lead the way.

ALLOW THE UNIVERSE TO SUPPORT YOU

Being a Super Attractor means remembering that you are an extension of the Universal energy. You are one with God and the Universe. You are love. When you are in joy, faith, and wonder, you can feel that connection fully. Each method in this book has brought you closer to reclaiming your Super Attractor connection. The goal is to get into a state of receptivity and allow. In a state of nonresistance, you can allow the Universal flow of well-being to support you. This is what Abraham-Hicks call "the art of allowing." To practice the art of allowing, begin by recognizing whether you're allowing the stream of well-being to move through you or not.

In this moment are you allowing love, joy, and well-being, or are you resisting it?

When you're allowing, you'll feel mentally clear and serene, and you'll have great faith. When you're not allowing, you'll feel aggravated, sad, guilty, frustrated, controlling, and even depressed. The emotions you feel indicate whether you're connected to your Super Attractor power. Negative thoughts and emotions embody low vibrations that keep you from letting the Universe support you. Abraham-Hicks suggest that when you say, "I really don't want that," you're becoming a match for what you don't want. If, for instance, you're constantly thinking about the potential of being fired from your job, your energy will be fearful, panicked, needy, and out of control. That energy sends out a message of fear to your employer (consciously or unconsciously) that you're not right for the position. Your incessant fearful thought of losing your job has the ability to manifest into form. Therefore, our work is to slow down the energy behind our negative thoughts by surrendering to the practices in this book. Each time you say a prayer, ask the Universe for help, choose again, or simply distract yourself from a negative thought, you're getting closer to your aligned state. Make your good-feeling thoughts and energy such a high priority that the feeling of well-being becomes natural to you. The goal is to allow well-being to flow through you in a nonresistant way. The art of allowing is the art of letting in what you want—health, wealth, joy, and love.

When you allow the Universal force of well-being to move through you, you can easily receive signs and guidance from the Universe. Maybe you begin to hear songs, receive messages from friends, and even sense intuitive direction from your own inner voice of wisdom. This divine guidance comes fast when you allow.

Your ego will likely resist this at first and try to control. But the more you accept that feeling good is the goal, then the easier it will be to allow that well-being to flow. You will begin to see that the more you allow, the more you attract.

When well-being flows, it feels as if invisible doors are opening for you and what you need is presented in the perfect time and order. When things seem to be held up or aren't happening the way you want, you intuitively know that there's something better on the way. Simply put, you allow. Embodying the energy of allowing brings grace, ease, and magnetic power to your overall presence. When you vibrate with this ease and magnetism, you are truly a Super Attractor.

Get into the habit of checking in with your emotions, recognizing when you're out of alignment, and then using any method from this book to come back to a receptive mode. Witness your emotions, surrender to well-being, and then do nothing and let the Universe show you what to do.

LET THE UNIVERSE CATCH UP WITH YOUR DREAMS

The final step in strengthening your faith in the Universe is to let the Universe catch up with your dreams. You may have big visions for your life. And maybe in this moment they feel far from reach. But I am writing this book to teach you that as long as you're aligned with empowering feelings, your desires will be a vibrational match for you. When you have faith in the Universe, it becomes safe to hold big visions even if you can't see them yet. When you make aligning with the Universe your priority, you can be unapologetic about your desires. It's not about how hard you push or how much you accomplish. Attracting your desires is about feeling good and having faith that the Universe is leading the way. Yes, of course you have to show up for your dreams. You have to take that job interview, go on that date, exercise your body. But when you feel good, your spiritually aligned actions are backed with the love of the Universe, and you can know you're attracting.

What it means to let the Universe catch up with your dreams is that you're willing to be patient. You're willing to surrender your timeline, your agenda, and your perceived needs. You're willing to have faith in a time frame beyond your own. Patience was my greatest virtue when manifesting my child. As soon as I truly accepted that the Universe had a better plan than my own, patience became natural. I embraced the journey, the healing, and the process. I trusted that my own timeline may not have been as healthy, easy, or seamless as the one the Universe had in store. And I was right. I can look back now and say *THANK YOU, UNIVERSE!* I am deeply grateful that I didn't get pregnant one day sooner. The moment I conceived was the perfect time in my life. I felt more supported than ever before. The Universe caught up to my dream in the most divine time for me to enjoy pregnancy and feel safe as I became a mother. For this I am truly grateful.

I know that when you too let the Universe guide you, you'll come to know this freedom. You'll look back and say, "Thank God that didn't happen sooner." And you'll feel blessed that you had the opportunity to learn, grow, and have fun along the way. That's what it's all about. Trust in a plan beyond your own, and let the Universe catch up with your dreams.

May the words in this chapter strengthen your faith, ease your need to control, and bring you closer to feeling free. Embrace these faithful steps and let the ever-present flow of love move through you effortlessly.

And many miracles will come. You'll be astonished by what you receive when you truly surrender to the Universe. In fact, the miracles are so great that you may even resist them at first. You may begin to think, "This is too good to be true." Or you might feel undeserving of the great gifts you receive. If you notice that resistance, don't worry. I've got your back. In the final chapter, I will guide you to accept greatness once and for all. This next chapter will address this resistance and give you clear direction on how to release it so that you can freely enjoy the richness of life! Follow my guidance, and surrender to the fact that you are a Super Attractor.

Chapter 11

UNWAVERING FAITH IN THE UNIVERSE

The beginning of my third trimester was one of the most magical times of my life. I fell even more madly in love with my husband, who took incredible care of me. I genuinely enjoyed my pregnancy, and I'd never felt healthier, sexier, or more alive. My business was thriving too. I'd attracted great partners, and my team was really stepping up. I was in the flow.

But one morning I got yanked out of the stream of well-being. I was having a casual conversation with a dear friend when she brought up some fearful stories about the third trimester of pregnancy. Usually I'd have the awareness to excuse myself from the conversation or politely ask the person to change the subject. But in this case the message was coming from someone I loved and trusted. She had nothing but my best interests in mind, but her precautions sent me into a fear spiral. I left the conversation and immediately began obsessing, trying to control, and hooking myself into fearful projections. Just when I thought I was truly flowing with the positive momentum of the Universe, I was faced with my ego's resistance to all the love and positivity I'd cultivated. Stuck in a fear spiral, I started calling all my doctor friends for advice and Googling symptoms and stories. Before I even realized it, I was back in the fear of my body, and I'd weakened my spiritual connection.

At first it was hard to see what was truly going on. It's so easy to forget about the ego's nasty tricks! I got caught up in the drama and fears of the world, temporarily separating from my Super Attractor power. I was knocked out of alignment with the love of the Universe, and I'd turned my back on faith. To make matters worse, I started to believe that my obsession with these negative stories was going to manifest them in my life. My fear of manifesting the problem only exacerbated it. I was caught in a web of fear, and I'd let my ego take me down.

How did this happen? How did I go so wrong so fast?

What happened was that when I got aligned with the Universe, life got good. Really good. As the Law of Attraction would have it, my focus on love and faith led me to what I truly desired. But fear—the ego—cannot survive in that light. And while I've done a lot of work to weaken the voice of fear, it still can grab me when things get good. *A Course in Miracles* says, "The ego is afraid of the spirit's joy, because once you have experienced it you will withdraw all protection from the ego, and become totally without investment in fear." In the presence of spirit's joy, the ego swooped in and convinced me that, actually, it was all *too good* to be true.

This fear spiral went on for more than two weeks. I couldn't get through the day without feeling caught up in the drama in my mind. I kept bringing up my fears to my husband, and I couldn't sleep through the night. Finally I hit bottom with the drama. It was four in the morning, and I couldn't sleep because I was consumed by my fear and anxiety. I got out of bed and went into the living room to meditate. I started my meditation with a prayer: *Universe,*

I recognize that I'm out of alignment. I am ready to be released from this fear. I choose love instead. Then I closed my eyes and repeated the mantra *I choose love instead.* I sat in stillness, repeating this mantra over and over, for several minutes. *I choose love instead. I choose love instead. I choose love instead.* Eventually I lost track of the mantra and fell into a deep state of peaceful stillness. I was quickly realigned with the Universe.

After a few minutes of marinating in this loving stillness, I heard a loud inner voice speak up and say, "Fear is a guide back to love." These words brought me instant relief. My Higher Self was giving me permission to forgive my fear and use it as a vehicle to return to love. This message reminded me that in any moment I can choose again and that I don't have to fear my fear. From this moment forward, I accepted a new story. I accepted my faith in the Universe, and I chose to commit to love. I decided to fully realign with my faith in my health, the strength of my baby, and the truth I knew to be real. I forgave my friend for igniting this fear in me, and I found gratitude for this powerful lesson.

Accepting fear shines light on it. The instant that I accepted my fear as a guide back to love, I was able to release its grip. I could see fear as an opportunity to strengthen my faith, as a temporary distraction rather than a permanent reality. I accepted that fear was my choice, and I could choose again in any moment.

This experience happened at the perfect time to help me realign with love before the end of my pregnancy. It also allowed me to conclude this book by reminding you of how easy it is to resist love when life gets good. As you follow the methods in this book, you'll feel the love of the Universe flow through your entire life. Beautiful synchronicities will show up, support will surround you, and you'll feel a profound connection to a higher power. But it's very possible that the voice of fear may speak up in the background to try to interrupt your flow. You may find yourself denying your greatness and forgetting about your spiritual connection. You may revert to controlling patterns, forget about your spiritual guides, and lose sight of the strength of the Universe. You might even be afraid to feel good.

If this happens, and the voice of fear tries to convince you that it's *too good to be true,* don't freak out. Return to this chapter, and follow my guidance. You don't have to fear your fear. You can use it as a way to get closer to love. Witness your fear when it shows up, and follow my guidance below to stay in alignment and strengthen your positive expectation of all the greatness that will continue to show up for you!

HONOR YOUR FEAR AS A GUIDE BACK TO LOVE

There's no reason to run from or deny your fear. In fact, this only gives it more momentum. Instead, be the gentle witness of any fearful projections that get in the way of your Super Attractor faith. It's possible that fear will jump in and try to interfere whenever life really starts to flow or you manifest a big dream. You are on a journey toward accepting miracles in your life. Any journey that involves changing deep-rooted habits will have bumps along the way. Fear is one of the nastiest habits of all, and it won't disappear overnight. Know that it will show up, and choose to change the way you see it.

You can choose to see your moments of fear as beautiful contrast. Fear is a gentle reminder of what you *don't* want, and therefore it helps you clarify what you *do* want. When you notice a fearful thought arise, you can choose again. Just witness the thoughts and feelings, and revisit the Choose Again Method to redirect your focus:

1. Notice the fear.

Notice when your fearful thoughts start sabotaging your positive flow, and ask yourself, "How do I feel right now?" Let yourself feel whatever is coming up for you.

2. Forgive the thought.

Forgive your fearful thoughts, and celebrate your desire to shift back to feeling good! You can say out loud to yourself, "I forgive this thought, and I know it is not real."

3. Choose again.

Answer this question: "What is the best-feeling thought I can find right now?" Then ask the Universe for support as you lean toward thoughts that feel good. Take your time to reach for positive thoughts about what you want and how you want to feel.

You can always rely on the Choose Again Method to help redirect your thoughts. If fear has you in a headlock, and choosing a more positive thought seems far from reach, you can stay in Step 2 of the Choose Again Method and simply forgive the thought. Forgiving the thought shifts you to an energy of acceptance rather than resistance. When you forgive the fearful thought, you're acknowledging that your fear isn't your truth. Forgiving your fear gives you permission to return to love when you're ready. Accepting a more positive and empowering relationship to fear is the fastest way to dissolve it.

Don't be afraid of fear getting in the way of your manifesting. You are now so aligned with your Super Attractor power that in any moment you can shift your energy and realign. The instances of fear, even if they last several days, will never actually disconnect you from your positive flow. You just have to remember to release your fear and realign.

Make this your mantra: *In any moment I can release my fear and realign with my Super Attractor power.*

EMBRACE A NEW BASELINE

As you start to feel better, you will need to embrace the idea that you can have a new baseline for your happiness. When you have a new baseline for your happiness, you accept that it's safe to feel good, it's natural to thrive, and your desires can flow to you easily. With your new baseline for happiness, you give yourself permission to feel good and attract what you want. You'll no longer have to move in and out of faith. You'll stop waiting for it all to come crashing down, and you'll become unapologetic about how good you feel. You'll no longer resist your greatness.

For years I struggled with feeling like the victim of my traumatic memories, addictive patterns, and stories from the past. But as I grew to accept a new normal and trust that it was good to feel good, I needed a new baseline for my happiness. I had to give myself permission to release my victim story and choose to live a miraculous life!

Take a moment to read this beautiful passage from *A Course in Miracles*:

> Can you imagine what a state of mind without illusions is? How it would feel? Try to remember when there was a time—perhaps a minute, maybe even less— when nothing came to interrupt your peace; when you were certain you were loved and safe. Then try to picture what it would be like to have that moment be extended to the end of time and to eternity. Then let the sense of quiet that you felt be multiplied a hundred times, and then be multiplied another hundred more.

This can be your new normal. You can live in a world without illusion, where nothing can interrupt your peace.

The more you heal the habit of fear and embrace the habit of love, the more happiness will become normal for you. Let your inner sense of quiet multiply each day as you strengthen your faith in spiritual guidance and the love of the Universe. Become more and more certain that you are loved and safe each time you call on your guides or angels for help. Know that nothing can interrupt your peace when you claim your Super Attractor power. Accept your new baseline today.

BE HAPPY IN ANTICIPATION OF WHAT'S COMING

To stay synchronized with the Universe, we have to continuously remind ourselves to accept that our positive energy is always supported. When we're happy in anticipation of what's coming, we expect miracles, feel comfortable in the positive flow, and no longer resist the love of the Universe. We remain grateful for all that is, even when things don't seem to be working out. I once heard someone in an Al-Anon recovery group say, "Gratitude doesn't mean we have to be happy about everything, but grateful for the lessons." We can accept that even the tough moments are divine lessons to guide us back to love. We can choose to perceive all of life, from the positivity to the challenges, through the same lens of love. This perception of life comes when we accept that we are entitled to miracles.

Living with happy anticipation of what's coming clears the path for solutions in all situations, even the difficult ones. Being in alignment is all that is required for you to anticipate the miraculous. When you strengthen your faith in the Universe and amplify the momentum behind your desires, you can look forward to positive outcomes. It's not always easy in a world filled with fear, but when you accept that feeling good begets more goodness, then you can expect the Universal support that's always available to you.

I once saw a poster that said, "Faith isn't hoping that God will help you. Faith is knowing that help is on the way." When we claim our desires, we must trust that the Universe is picking up what we're putting out. We don't have to hope for support to show up; we can know with certainty that it's on the way. Hopefully by now you have experienced the speed with which the Universe can show up to support you. You may have received a sign from a spirit guide, felt instant relief upon saying a prayer, or even seen your desire realized in full form. Celebrate the support of the Universe, and expect more of it. Everyone has the capacity to receive miracles when they choose to send out a positive signal.

Trust that your positive energy is enough to allow your desires to show up in your life. When you have faith in your power to attract, you can be happy in anticipation of what's coming. Instead of worrying about the future, you can know that all is well when you're aligned in the present. It's the moments of alignment that focus your point of attraction toward exactly what you desire. Give yourself permission to get excited about your desires and feel your way into the energy of all that you're creating. Know that feeling good is itself a radical act of creation.

CARE ABOUT HOW YOU FEEL

Above all else, care about how you feel. Of course we all want to feel good, but we don't consciously think thoughts and take actions that make us feel good. In fact, we often do the opposite. Caring about how you feel means that you become more deliberate about the words you choose, the thoughts you think, and the actions you take. It means that you go out of your way to realign your energy with love.

When you care about how you feel, you maintain an energy of receptivity. From that place of receptivity, all you have to do is think about what you desire, and the Universe will deliver. Pay attention to what happens when you feel good. How do other people respond to you? How quickly do issues get resolved? And how easy is it for you to attract what you desire?

My favorite method for directing my good-feeling emotions is something I call Daily Design. It's easy to do. Each morning, when you wake up, open your Super Attractor journal and answer these four questions:

How do I want to feel today?

Who do I want to be today?

What do I want to receive today?

What do I want to give today?

Take your time answering each question as specifically as possible. This is a process of co-creating your day with the Universe. See yourself enjoying the completion of a task that you've been avoiding. Envision yourself having positive encounters with everyone, from your family to your co-workers. Picture your morning commute going smoothly. Design your day exactly how you want it to be, and have fun writing about it.

The process of designing your day and writing it down is a powerful way to focus on exactly how you want to feel. Make the Daily Design Method a morning habit, and you'll notice that things begin to work out exactly as you planned—or that something even better happens. People will respond to you more positively. By caring about how you feel and directing your focus toward positive visualizations, you allow the

Universe to support you. The more you practice good-feeling thoughts, the more your ability to receive grows.

BE CONSCIOUS OF YOUR ENERGY

Another way to be sure you're caring about how you feel is to pay attention to the interactions you have with others. Remember that we are all vibrational beings, so it's easy to pick up what other people are putting out. You may not even realize it when someone has an energetic hold on you. But you can become much more aware of the way other people's energy affects you. Pay attention to how you feel around certain people, and do your part to be conscious of your own energy. You don't have to shun or judge people for having low vibes. Instead, choose to create clear boundaries, ask to change the subject of a conversation, or even politely remove yourself from a situation that's lowering your vibrational stance. It's your responsibility to take care of your energy. And remember that other people's energy is *not* your responsibility. You are not responsible for other people's happiness. Every individual has the power to shift their own life, and you can't do it for them. If you try to force positivity onto someone, you'll feel drained. The best thing you can do for them is to feel good. When you feel good, you elevate the energy around you, and others pick up on it. You can trust that your good-feeling emotions will bring you both resolution.

SEEK RELIEF RATHER THAN SOLUTIONS

As a Super Attractor, you know that your good-feeling vibrations lead to positive experiences. Begin to accept and expect that the more positivity you put into your life, the more supported you will feel. This positive expectation will give you a sense of freedom and ease in all your day-to-day experiences. For instance, maybe you have a falling-out with a friend and are tempted to find an immediate solution by fighting back or trying to fix the issue. But instead you can follow this guidance from Abraham-Hicks and seek relief instead of a solution. As a result of seeking relief, you achieve a good-feeling vibration, and soon the solution is presented to you.

How do you seek relief? You can do this by praying, repeating a positive affirmation, or even by distracting yourself with any activity that brings you joy. You have the power to redirect your focus off the need to find a solution. Sometimes I even ask myself, "Would I rather be right or happy?" This question always helps me return to the truth of what I want—to feel good! When I make happiness my priority over being right and seeking solutions, I can instantly return to an energy of ease. Try this every time you're tempted to fix a situation, and look for relief instead. The moment you find relief, solutions will find you.

THE PRACTICE OF NONINTERFERENCE

The practice of noninterference is crucial when living as a Super Attractor. We can attract so much more when we get out of the way. Try your best not to control your circumstances, but instead allow them to unfold naturally. You've done great work getting your energy into alignment. Now trust that your alignment is enough to receive. When you're in sync with your true nature, you can relax, be at peace, and allow the fullness and joy of the Universe to flow through you. Allow people to support you. Allow miracles to unfold.

As you might expect, your ego will want to resist this. When something you care about is on the line, you'll want to step in, play God, and try to make things go your way. Your conscious nonresistance is required to stay in the flow with the Universe. Each day, make it a priority to release resistance a little more. When you notice yourself second-guessing something, offer it up to the Universe through prayer. When you catch yourself judging others, swiftly choose a more loving topic. If you wake up feeling misaligned, turn to your journal and practice the Daily Design Method. Or return to your practice from Chapter 10: do nothing, and let the Universe show you what to do. All of these practices will help you get out of the way and release resistance. Every method in this book is designed to help you get into a state of allowing.

Pay attention to your emotions, and let them indicate your level of resistance. If you notice your emotional stance is out of sync with love, that tells you that you're not allowing well-being to flow. Don't let your emotions become misguided. Return to the emotional scale and gently guide yourself back to joy. Stay committed to returning to love, and you can trust that you're allowing. Find a way to hold yourself in harmony with the emotions of well-being so that the support and love of the Universe can flow through you in a nonresistant way.

Abraham-Hicks refer to this as the art of letting in what you want—allowing health, wealth, well-being, love. Abraham-Hicks emphasize that there's no source of sickness; rather, there's not letting in of wellness. There's no source of lack; there's only not letting in of abundance. Shift your perception from what you think you're lacking to what you're not allowing. You'll come to see that your perceived lack is a reflection of your resistance to the love of the Universe. Take small actions daily to release your resistance and let in all that you desire.

It's time to allow the abundant love of the Universe to flow. Give yourself permission to feel good and dream big. Don't undermine your desires and visions with limiting beliefs and words. Claim that you can be and have what you desire. Love is available to you now. You can resist it or allow it. This is the time to allow.

COMMIT TO BEING A SUPER ATTRACTOR

As I complete this book, I'm days away from delivering my child. I woke up this morning, and I knew this was the perfect time to conclude our journey together. Here I am in the midst of the greatest uncertainty I've ever faced. My labor and delivery are largely out of my control, my doctor loves to caution me that I'm giving birth at "39 years young," and my life is about to change forever.

Instead of letting the fears of my age or my labor consume me, I turned to my spiritual practice and asked for a clear sign to reassure me I am making the right decisions. The sign I chose was a cardinal because earlier that week I'd noticed my doctor's necktie was adorned with cardinals. I asked him about it, and he said, "I love birds, and cardinals are one of my favorites." Given that I was asking for guidance related to my doctor and my labor, I chose the cardinal as my sign. Over the next few days, I was encouraged to make major decisions about my labor—all the while waiting for my cardinal to appear to assure me I was on the right path. I remained patient and receptive, educating myself on my options. Finally, and without having received my sign, I came to a plan that nevertheless felt good to me. I texted my friend and spiritual running buddy MaryAnn and shared my plans. An hour later, she texted me back: "This sounds great. And the moment I looked at your text, I noticed a cardinal right on my car window. This seems like a sign for you." Amazingly, MaryAnn had no idea that the cardinal was my sign or even that I was looking for a sign at all! Spirit worked through her to reassure me that I was on the right path. Being in clear communication with the Universe is the most awe-inspiring experience. It's a gift to know I'm being guided.

In the midst of this uncertainty, societal pressure, and fear stories, I have two choices. I can let my ego take hold, or I can remember that I am a Super Attractor. Today there's only one choice that I will tolerate. I choose to be a Super Attractor and have unwavering faith in the Universe. I choose happiness as my baseline, I choose positive expectation, I choose joyful anticipation of what's coming, I choose to care about how I feel, I choose to seek relief rather than solutions, and most importantly, I choose to practice noninterference. I turn over my will to the care of the spiritual guidance I've grown to rely on, and today I surrender even more.

There is maybe no greater surrender than the birth of a child. For this I'm grateful. This new experience that I embark on will be my greatest opportunity to strengthen my faith in the Universe. This is my chance to completely release control, visualize my desire, feel good, trust, and allow. I have an opportunity to live the practices in this book in a whole new way.

Feeling into the uncertainty of my labor and the magnitude of becoming a mother, I return to the messages in this book. It feels good to know there's a world beyond limitation and doubt. It feels soothing to know that I can surrender my labor and delivery to the care of the Universe, the angels, and my guides. And it feels safe to surrender my plans and trust in a spiritual guidance system. Today I make this commitment to you, my friends. I commit to allow the Universe to show me what to do. I commit to stay in the flow with positive thoughts and maintain the momentum of joy. And I commit to welcome my child into this world with fearless grace and ease, knowing that I am a Super Attractor.

Make this commitment to yourself today. Say out loud, "I am committed to being a Super Attractor." Let your fear be your guide back to love. When you're faced with challenges, know that there is a plan beyond your own. Allow yourself to feel supported and guided. And know that you're making a major contribution to the world by choosing to live in the light. Each time you lift the veil and step into the light, the world shines brighter. Continue to make love your priority, believe in the Universe, and follow the guidance you receive. It's your choice to live a new life filled with joy, grace, ease, and strength. It's your choice to have fun, be well, and attract what you desire. It's your choice to be a Super Attractor.

AFTERWORD

I planned to deliver this manuscript to my publisher on December 18, 2018, the day before I was scheduled for an induction. My doctor had spent countless hours convincing me to deliver my baby at 40 weeks because of my age. I resisted his suggestions at first, but in the end I surrendered the plan to the Universe and asked for a sign. As soon as I received the sign of the cardinal, I knew that it was safe to go ahead with the plan for induction.

Then on the night of December 17, I lay in bed with my big belly, back pain, and swollen legs. I was reading over this manuscript and making my final edits. I felt so good reading these pages! Once again, this book guided me back to love and strengthened my faith in the Universe. Days before I was meant to be induced, I was able to release my fear and return to faith that I was being guided.

After an hour of reading, I stood up to get a drink. To my great surprise, the moment I stood up, my water broke. I was thrilled! I yelled down to Zach that it was time to go, and I grabbed my hospital bag. My baby was on his way!

The delivery I had thought I was destined for was far different from the miracle I received. I wanted my son to come on his own time, and once again the Universe delivered. For months I'd held a vision of the labor I wanted to have. I saw myself free from fear, moving through each surge with ease, and peacefully delivering my child. I held this vision and surrendered it to the Universe.

We calmly headed to the hospital that night, filled with excited anticipation but also a great sense of peace. The following morning I went into labor. I live in a country town with a small regional hospital. As I had envisioned, I was the only person laboring in the maternity ward. I had two amazing doulas, six loving nurses, a caring obstetrician, and my incredible husband there to support me.

Outside my hospital window was a view of the bright blue sky and the rolling hills of the countryside. I played my mantra music and lit votive candles to make the space serene. I sang the word "ahh" as I moved through each surge. "Ahh," the Universal sound for God, was what instinctively came through me. I set up a shrine across from my bed with images of the baby in the perfect position for delivery and another image of a flower opening, representing the cervix at 10 centimeters dilated. Every hour, I meditated with my doulas, listening to mantras and gazing at the images. I held visions of my cervix opening and stayed calm through every surge. Each time the doctor checked my cervix, I committed to meditate before the next surge to help my body open up more. He'd return in an hour, and I'd be dilated another centimeter, closer to birthing my baby. My meditation, affirmation, and visualization guided me through 14 hours of labor. By 1 A.M. the following day, my son, Oliver, entered the world with grace and ease. When the doctor gently set him on my chest, I looked at my baby and said, "I know you." It was as if we'd been together for many lifetimes. This was the best day of my life and my greatest manifestation.

As I write this afterword, Oliver is asleep next to me on my sofa. He is seven weeks old and has already proven to be my greatest spiritual teacher. He has brought me a new sense of presence, patience, and most of all an opportunity to deepen my faith in the Universe. He is my greatest desire made manifest. I know that the birth of this soul is a reflection of my willingness to be guided and my trust in a plan beyond my own.

The Universe always has a plan far better than we do. The three years I spent trying to conceive taught me the gift of surrender. I focused on feeling good and strengthened my faith in the Universe to deliver my son at the perfect time. Looking back, I can see how there was no better time than now for me to become a mother. Each day I return to these practices to remind myself that anything is possible when I'm aligned with my Super Attractor power. I am committed to living these truths and instilling them in my child. The greatest lesson I can teach him is that when he's aligned with the power of love, he will live a miraculous life.

Our willingness to surrender to the Universe is what allows an invisible guidance to take over. When we surrender, we realign with faith, and in that alignment we are shown where to go and what to do. We can relax and trust in the unfolding. Be proud of your commitment to these practices, and celebrate your internal shifts. May these pages guide your path and clear space for the Universe to midwife your dreams.

ACKNOWLEDGMENTS

I thank and honor the team of human angels who helped me bring this book to life. My agents, Scott Hoffman and Steve Troha, thank you for guiding me throughout the publishing process. I thank Reid Tracy, Patty Gift, Michelle Pilley, Anne Barthel, and the entire Hay House family for believing in me and my work. I'm grateful for my newest publishing relationship with Stacy Creamer at Audible. May the audiobook serve many souls. I could never launch a book without my devoted PR team, Sarah Hall PR. Thank you, Jessica Reda and Sarah Hall, for always making sure the message is spread far and wide. I am deeply grateful for the work of Esther Hicks and Abraham—thank you for the inspiration. I thank my editor, Katie Karas. Katie, you are my literary partner and dear friend, and it's an honor to have you by my side. I thank my team for holding space for me to be creative and feel supported. I thank my event planner, Anette Sharvit, for making sure every single book gets signed throughout the tour. I thank my personal development team and friends, Kachina Myers, Tammy Valicenti, Aviva Romm, Teri Goetz, Aimee Raupp, MaryAnn DiMarco, Alexandra Sacks, and Lori Leyden. Thank you all for helping me heal so that I can rise up. Finally, I thank my husband and best friend, Zach. Z, you are the greatest business partner, husband, friend, and father. Oliver is blessed to call you Dad.

ABOUT THE AUTHOR

For over fifteen years, Gabrielle Bernstein has been transforming lives—including her own. The #1 *New York Times* best-selling author has penned eight books including *The Universe Has Your Back, Super Attractor,* and the latest, her first Audible Original, *You Are the Guru.* What started as hosting intimate conversations with twenty people in her New York City apartment, Gabby has grown into speaking to tens of thousands in sold-out venues throughout the world.

Gabby was featured on Oprah's *SuperSoul Sunday* as a "next-generation thought leader." The Oprah Winfrey Network chose Gabby to be part of the "SuperSoul 100," a dynamic group of trailblazers whose vision and life's work are bringing a higher level of consciousness to the world. *The New York Times* identified Gabby as "a new role model." She co-hosted the Guinness World Records' largest guided meditation with Deepak Chopra, and appears regularly as an expert on *Today* and *Good Morning America* among other publications. Gabby connects with her community through her books, her Miracle Membership, the Spirit Junkie app, social media, podcasts, masterclasses, digital workshops and e-courses, and live events. To learn more and experience it yourself, visit gabbybernstein.com.

Hay House Titles of Related Interest

YOU CAN HEAL YOUR LIFE, the movie,
starring Louise Hay & Friends
(available as a 1-DVD program, an expanded 2-DVD set,
and an online streaming video)
Learn more at www.hayhouse.com/louise-movie

THE SHIFT, the movie, starring Dr. Wayne W. Dyer
(available as a 1-DVD program, an expanded 2-DVD set,
and an online streaming video)
Learn more at www.hayhouse.com/the-shift-movie

***

THE UNIVERSE HAS YOUR BACK: Transform Fear to Faith

MIRACLES NOW: 108 Life-Changing Tools for Less Stress,
More Flow, and Finding Your True Purpose

SUPER ATTRACTOR: A 52-Card Deck

THE UNIVERSE HAS YOUR BACK: A 52-Card Deck

MIRACLES NOW: A 62-Card Deck

All of the above are available at your local bookstore,
or may be ordered by contacting Hay House (see next page).

***

We hope you enjoyed this Hay House book. If you'd like to receive our online catalog featuring additional information on Hay House books and products, or if you'd like to find out more about the Hay Foundation, please contact:

Hay House, Inc., P.O. Box 5100, Carlsbad, CA 92018-5100
(760) 431-7695 or (800) 654-5126
(760) 431-6948 (fax) or (800) 650-5115 (fax)
www.hayhouse.com® • www.hayfoundation.org

———

Published in Australia by: Hay House Australia Pty. Ltd.,
18/36 Ralph St., Alexandria NSW 2015
Phone: 612-9669-4299 • *Fax:* 612-9669-4144
www.hayhouse.com.au

Published in the United Kingdom by: Hay House UK, Ltd.,
The Sixth Floor, Watson House, 54 Baker Street, London W1U 7BU
Phone: +44 (0)20 3927 7290 • *Fax:* +44 (0)20 3927 7291
www.hayhouse.co.uk

Published in India by: Hay House Publishers India,
Muskaan Complex, Plot No. 3, B-2, Vasant Kunj, New Delhi 110 070
Phone: 91-11-4176-1620 • *Fax:* 91-11-4176-1630
www.hayhouse.co.in

———

Access New Knowledge.
Anytime. Anywhere.

Learn and evolve at your own pace
with the world's leading experts.

www.hayhouseU.com

CONTINUE YOUR JOURNEY OF

MANIFESTING MIRACLES

SUPER ATTRACTOR

Each card in this beautiful deck offers an inspiring mantra to guide you on your path to manifesting your dreams. Use the cards to help you act in alignment with the Universe, connect to your Super Attractor power, and attract your greatest desires.

HAY HOUSE   www.hayhouse.com

MORE RESOURCES FROM

GABRIELLE BERNSTEIN

SUPER ATTRACTOR JOURNAL

In this gorgeously illustrated journal, you'll find plenty of writing space to document your miracles and strengthen your spiritual connection. You'll also discover practical tools—including 8 interactive lessons—to help you implement Gabrielle Bernstein's powerful teachings and activate your own Super Attractor abilities.

 www.hayhouse.com